Party Propaganda
Under Queen Anne

The University
of Georgia Press

James O. Richards

Party Propaganda Under Queen Anne

The General Elections of 1702-1713

Library of Congress Catalogue Card Number: 79-184778
International Standard Book Number: 0-8203-0273-2

The University of Georgia Press, Athens 30601

Printed in the United States of America
by Heritage Printers, Inc.
Charlotte, North Carolina 28202

For Jaimee, Paige, and Barbara

Illustrations

The illustrations are in the order listed on a signature following page 120.

Contents

Acknowledgments

The collections from which I drew the pamphlets and periodicals used in this study are in the British Museum, the Bodleian Library, the Library of the University of Illinois (Urbana), the Newberry Library, the Boston Public Library, and the libraries of Yale University, Harvard University, McGill University, and Columbia University. Miss Isabelle Grant, formerly rare book librarian of the University of Illinois, was especially helpful to me during the search for the publications I needed.

A mere thank-you seems to be an inadequate way to repay the efforts of Professor Maurice Lee, Jr., who proposed the study and guided me through the first version of it. I deeply appreciate his encouragement during the revision for publication. Professors Henry L. Snyder and W. A. Speck were most kind in replying to my queries. Three other people have given more than all the others—my wife, Barbara, who typed what must have seemed an endless succession of drafts, and my two daughters, Jaimee and Paige, whom this little book has cost a lot of family time and fun.

James O. Richards

Macon Junior College
Macon, Georgia

Introduction

i

A study of election propaganda under Queen Anne has wider implications than the title and temporal scope may seem initially to suggest. It touches on a question important to anyone with a taste for party politics and an interest in history: What is the nature of party or what constitutes the basis for party? The indispensable fabric of party is a nexus of broad attitudes toward important, lasting issues, a collection of interlocking assumptions, of dispositions regarding fundamental public matters. These form the theoretical or ideological underpinning of party out of which party propaganda comes. But what men have considered a full definition of party has not remained constant.

English political parties as organized bodies of men struggling for office and its perquisites, standing on opposing platforms and seeking the votes of a democratic electorate, are little over a century old. Not until the House of Commons became the cockpit of political struggles, as it did in Elizabethan and Stuart times, could the development of parties even begin. Even so prior to Edmund Burke's classic apologia for political parties in the late eighteenth century, *Thoughts on the Causes of the Present Discontents*, no one dared argue publicly that organized groups justifiably could seek control of the government. Any intention to organize for capturing the reins of government was subversive, even antimonarchical. Government was still the king's job, not Parliament's, and men had not yet learned to distinguish between the king reigning and the king ruling. They were learning to make this distinction during the reigns of the first three Georges when government became too onerous and complex for immediate royal attention. And Burke, observing that the ruling of the kingdom was actually in the hands of the king's ministers, argued that planning to secure control of the government was not treasonous but perfectly legitimate. At the century's end "party" as an organized body was no longer a reprehensible notion; men began openly to countenance its function in politics.

By the end of the nineteenth century the parliamentary and party system had developed into forms substantially as they are today. Those organized bodies working to control the government were, by then, tightly disciplined into two large parties with distinctive programs and policies. In the constituencies local associations nominated candidates and closely watched their behavior if they were elected; central offices disseminated propaganda on behalf of the party, coordinated efforts, and established communication among the party head and his parliamentary colleagues and the rank-and-file of the party. By then, too, the prime minister was the head of the largest party in Commons. Much of this was due to great leaders of the century, men who by strength of will and personality brought their lesser colleagues into the most functional means of governing the nation from Westminster. But much also was owed to the vastly increased numbers of voters who were enfranchised by the great reform acts of the century. Candidates who formerly had appealed to a rather limited electorate now had to work and plead for popular favor. In fact they became less important than the parties' programs since voters were more interested in what parties proposed to do for them than in the merits of rival candidates.

If political parties as disciplined units are relatively recent, what was party in the early eighteenth century before political parties became tightly organized bodies? Here we plunge immediately into a scholarly controversy which involves the subject of this book and which really thrusts us up against the crucial question raised at the beginning: What is the nature of party? There are two views of English politics during the early eighteenth century: one shaped in the main by scholars of the 1920s and 1930s which assumes that there were two parties, "Whig" and "Tory," contesting with each other for political power;[1] and the view of Robert Walcott (and perhaps presciently labeled by him the "heresy") in which he insists that the two-party explanation is misleading and that party politics are best explained not simply by reference to Whig or Tory labels but also to basic political connections—seven to be exact—headed by the court and influential peers and gentry.[2] Walcott drew on the insights of one of the most seminal historical minds of recent times, Sir Lewis Namier, whose researches into the middle period of the eighteenth century convinced him that one could describe party activity of that period without using the traditional "Whigs" or "Tories" but by identifying and studying the activities of political opportunism. Walcott, attempting to transport the Namierian method and insights backward to the beginnings of the eighteenth century, proposed that in preference to the older view of scholars, students of the period should consider finely graded variations of the conven-

1. For works representative of this view see W. T. Morgan, *English Political Parties and Leaders in the Reign of Queen Anne, 1702–1710* (1920); G. M. Trevelyan, *England under the Stuarts* (1949); Keith Feiling, *A History of the Tory Party, 1640–1714* (1924).

2. Walcott's thesis is much more fully developed in *English Politics in the Early Eighteenth Century* (1956) than in his earlier essay on the same subject, "English Party Politics, (1688–1714)," in *Essays in Modern English History in Honor of Wilbur Cortez Abbott* (1941).

tional Tory and Whig alignments: Court Tories, Court Whigs, Country Tories, Country Whigs, and the like.

Walcott's work, though monographic, has stirred the controversy over the meaning of party because its critics have charged that Walcott denies the motive force of political ideas in searching for the quantitative features of party activities—how men voted in the House of Commons, what their backgrounds and occupations were, who their relatives were, and similar questions. In the decades since the publication of Walcott's study critics have dissented from his thesis without being able to show conclusively how he was wrong. Recently, however, J. H. Plumb and G. S. Holmes have demolished many of Walcott's arguments.[3] While admitting that he had some things of value to say—the analysis of the Parliament of 1701 and of factionalism within Tory ranks—Plumb and especially Holmes have produced more than enough evidence to vindicate the traditional assumption that there were two major political parties overarching any other factions and that a majority of Englishmen would have placed themselves within one of these two major groupings. Holmes has shown, for instance, that many of the trappings of party, in the modern sense of the term, even existed in the early eighteenth century. There were party leaders and party organizations. In Commons men almost invariably voted along Whig or Tory lines. Early eighteenth-

3. Plumb's *The Growth of Political Stability in England, 1675–1725* (1967) is the strongest assault. Holmes's *British Politics in the Age of Anne* (1967) is more thorough. Pages 2–9, 38–39, and 327–334 sum up much of Holmes's disagreement with Walcott's views. To these two works must be added the recent study by W. A. Speck, *Whig and Tory: The Struggle in the Constituencies, 1701–1715* (1970), which was published as my own work was going to press. I used Mr. Speck's Oxford dissertation, "The House of Commons, 1702–1714: A Study in Political Organization" (1965), on part of which his book was based.

century parties were not monolithic structures, but it is clear from Holmes's work that they were not unstructured and meaningless entities as Walcott had suggested.

Given the disarray of Walcott's arguments the controversy may begin to subside. But there are still many facets of early eighteenth-century political party life which have not been studied: prominent among them are election propaganda and its instigation, dissemination, and influence. G. S. Holmes has sketched the broad lines of Whiggism and Toryism in Anne's reign, but no one has analyzed the hundreds of election pamphlets, broadsides, poems, and periodical issues for what they tell us about political thought during crucial periods of party activity. Almost all this literature falls within the two traditional ideological perspectives of Whiggism and Toryism so that it offers further evidence of the validity of the two-party interpretation of politics in the period. It appealed for votes on the basis of ideology, which constituted a large measure of what party meant in an age when party organization was mainly informal. Thus in studying election propaganda we discover some things essential to the idea of party and basic to the political behavior of men generally.

There are several reasons for choosing to study election propaganda rather than more general party propaganda. The five general elections of Anne's reign were not the only occasions for which propaganda was produced. It appeared in prodigious amounts during the intervals between elections, for example, during the occasional conformity crisis of 1702–1704 or the government's campaign to force the Allies to submit to British peace proposals in 1711–1712. But the value of analyzing election literature instead of samples of other party literature is that it was more broadly oriented: it argued the spectrum of issues rather than select ones. Treating the propaganda of five elections extending over a span of almost twelve years gives us the opportunity to observe the development of ideologies and of propaganda techniques over a period of prolific party journalism. And it provides occasions—election contests—for assessing the influence of ideologies and issues, difficult though it is to show their importance. There are problems attending any study involving public opinion, and before turning to the elections themselves we shall want to know what some of these problems are, as well as some antecedents to the party and ideological struggles of Anne's reign.

ii The answers to the problems of "public opinion" probably always lie in murky depths, and this is especially true for a work on party propaganda. The problems need to be raised, nonetheless, if for no other reason than to indicate by way of the negative what we do *not* know. Implied in our treatment of party propaganda is the existence of party presses, but we need to know who ordered the writing of election materials and what the relationships between party writers and leaders were before we can accurately speak of a "party press." For the writings we should know how many copies of each piece were published, how many constituencies each piece reached, how many readers there were in each constituency, and the impact this literature had on voters' decisions. What do we know? There are appropriate points in the election studies where one may consider these problems more carefully and fully, but the general picture of relationships between party leaders and writers contains more shadows than highlights. It is very clear that major writers such as Daniel Defoe and Jonathan Swift received instructions and hints about things to write, but we know little about other writers and their connections with leaders. And even in Defoe's and Swift's cases it is difficult to identify the pieces of propaganda they wrote. Political writers did not often sign their works. Such identification as we can make frequently must be on the basis of internal evidence or chance references to authorship in other sources.

There were real reasons for anonymity, since a writer risked jail or possibly death if his authorship was known or suspected by offended public authorities.[4] There was logic to anonymity, too, because of public distaste for partisanship. Knowledge that he had hired a writer to put forth Whig or Tory views probably was not the sort of revelation a party leader wanted. Again he might have wanted to avoid links that would have implicated him in any government prosecution of writers. Robert Harley, for instance, worked quietly to have Defoe released and pardoned on several occasions—once when his colleague as secretary of state was having Defoe prosecuted.[5] And Harley always made Defoe see him in secret.[6] Even Jonathan Swift, whose relations with the Harley–St. John ministry were not so secret, seems to have been allowed such public intimacy with ministers only as a sop to his vanity;[7] his case is unique. Harley also wanted to avoid committing himself to any one policy, and his secretiveness about many of his plans meant that even Defoe and Swift, whom he employed simultaneously, did not

4. See David Stevens, *Party Politics and English Journalism, 1702–1742* (1916), pp. 12–13, 32–34, and Laurence Hanson, *Government and the Press, 1695–1763* (1936), pp. 16–18, 58.

5. Stevens, pp. 48, 52.

6. Richard I. Cook, " 'Mr. *Examiner*' and 'Mr. *Review*': The Tory Apologetics of Swift and Defoe," pp. 127–146.

7. Ibid.

know the extent to which they were writing Harley's true intentions. Swift actually seems not to have known that Defoe worked for Harley.[8]

Suggestive of the secrecy, too, was the relationship of a minor writer, Stephen Whately, and Robert Walpole, a coming Whig leader of Anne's last years and the famous Sir Robert of later reigns. Whately's work for Walpole from 1710 to 1713 did not come to light until 1723 when he wrote trying to get help for a case in litigation and reminded Walpole of what he had done for him: among other things "the private Printing and Dispersing of several Papers wrote by the Best Pens against the Enemies of the Protestant Succession, particularly the Letter to the West Country Clothier, the Short History of the Parliament, and others with which I will not now take up Your Time."[9] So perhaps it is understandable that we have few hard facts about the relationship of party leaders and writers.

We can only speculate on skimpy evidence about the nature of the machinery by which party propaganda was disseminated. Some important leaders such as Harley and Walpole and Whig Junto lords were directly responsible for election propaganda, as we shall see later. The unity of party ideas and perspectives on issues bespeaks some central direction, even if only infrequent and clandestine meetings between party leaders and individual writers. By modern standards there was no "party press," but the cohesiveness and coherency in party writing suggest that the reason for these was more than coincidence. We go far beyond the evidence if we say there were central planning groups, but we are fairly safe if we assume that pro-

8. Ibid. See also Lawrence Poston, III, "Defoe and the Peace Campaign, 1710–1713: A Reconsideration," pp. 4–5.

9. Stevens, pp. 28–29.

paganda came from individual party writers who did not often collaborate, who knew only what they were working on and the men from whom they took their orders, or suggestions, as the case might be. The cohesiveness could follow from the traditional and essentially simple nature of many of the election issues and from leaders' suggestions.

How many copies of each writing were published and how many constituencies did each piece reach? Answers here must be even more vague because the evidence is more minuscule. We need statistics and have few, which follows from the secrecy with which pamphlets and periodicals were written and published. We are fortunate if we can identify the publisher of a piece, let alone obtain his records, if he kept any. So we have to use thin references and diverse sources to put together what little we have. Some pamphlets, we know, went through several editions in one year. Defoe's *True Born Englishman* went through twenty-one editions and approximately eighty thousand copies after its publication in 1701, a pamphlet attacking Dr. Sacheverell in 1710 sold sixty thousand copies in London alone, and Swift's *Conduct of the Allies* sold eleven thousand in two months.[10] So certain pamphlets sold as briskly as contemporary best sellers considering printing difficulties and the size of the population. For pamphlets cited in this study, however, such sales were not common, nor was more than one edition usual.[11] The circumstances of printing made it likely that several hundred (perhaps, on the high side, one to two

10. Alexandre Beljame, *Men of Letters and the English Public in the Eighteenth Century* (1948), p. 309.

11. It does seem, however, that twenty-one of the one hundred or so pamphlets I used for this study went through more than one edition. I computed this from William T. Morgan and Chloe S. Morgan, *Bibliography of British History, 1700–1715*, 5 vols. (1934–1942).

thousand) copies of any pamphlet would be cranked out to get a decent return from its sale price of a few pence. But this is sheer speculation.

For periodicals we do have some circulation figures. In mid-1704 nine newspapers were publishing almost forty-four thousand copies a week in single, biweekly, or triweekly issues. Of these, four papers were known for their partisanship, two of them, Defoe's *Review* and John Tutchin's *Observator*, for active propagandizing and electioneering. The *Post Boy*, nominally Tory, and the *Flying Post*, nominally Whig, published respectively nine thousand and twelve hundred copies weekly; the *Review* and *Observator*, eight hundred and two thousand. The *Review* became triweekly in 1705, and even if it did not increase its circulation each issue, which seems unlikely, it probably increased to twelve hundred with the third issue. By using a fragment of evidence for 1710 and the recent findings of Henry Snyder, we can compute a rough total of fifteen to sixteen thousand copies circulating weekly in 1710. The *Examiner*, *Whig-Examiner*, and *Medley* began in 1710. In 1713 the *British Merchant*, *Englishman*, and *Mercator* joined these partisan journals, and the *Review*, *Observator*, and *Medley* had ceased publication. So the total for that year might have been around twenty-two thousand copies weekly. I have not mentioned the *Rehearsal* (1704–1709) or the *Moderator* (1710) because there are no figures for them.[12]

In London itself virtually every partisan publication was sure to be noticed, but how far from London would pamphlets and papers get? Certainly many of them found their way to the counties and boroughs. Readers in the provinces, wanting

---

12. James R. Sutherland, "The Circulation of Newspapers and Literary Periodicals, 1700–1730," pp. 110–124; Henry L. Snyder, "The Circulation of Newspapers in the Reign of Queen Anne," pp. 206–235.

to know what was going on in the nation's cockpit, nagged their friends or M.P.'s in London to send news.[13] Even a lord important enough to get personal reports from the queen's ministers occasionally had to depend for his "usual entertainment," as he put it, on *Post Boys* and *Examiners*.[14] Members of Parliament had franking privileges in the postal system and were expected to get papers to the provinces as cheaply as possible for select subscribers.[15] For those who would use them for partisan purposes probably even the subscription was free. A parson in Scarborough, Yorkshire, gathered a coterie every Sunday evening to read the *Examiner* sent him by an M.P. from the borough and then carried it with him all week to use against the influence of the *Review* and *Observator* on his parishioners.[16] Swift in one of his letters to Stella noted a special printing of his *Conduct of the Allies* "to be sent in numbers into the country by great men, etc. who subscribe for hundreds."[17] And a writer to the *Examiner* began his letter by saying "I Am a Country Member, and constantly send a dozen of your Papers down to my Electors."[18]

Defoe seems to have tried in 1704 to set up a network to disperse the *Review* and pamphlets, a network which depended on local volunteer agents such as John Fransham of Norwich.

13. Geoffrey A. Cranfield, *The Development of the Provincial Newspaper, 1700–1760* (1962), p. 178.

14. Great Britain, Historical Manuscripts Commission, Report on the MSS of the Earl of Dartmouth, I, 296: the Earl of Jersey to the Earl of Dartmouth, August 9, 1710. Cited hereinafter as H.M.C., Dartmouth MSS.

15. Cranfield, p. 179.

16. Great Britain, Historical Manuscripts Commission, Report on the MSS of the Duke of Portland, IV, 641: J. Durden to Robert Harley, December 5, 1710. Cited hereinafter as H.M.C., Portland MSS.

17. *Journal to Stella* (1948), II, 441, December 18, 1711.

18. Richard I. Cook, "The Audience of Swift's Tory Tracts, 1710–1714," p. 39.

"As my purpose of writing is to furnish our Friends with arguments to defend the cause against a clamorous noisy Enemy, so it must be necessary that they should see them as much as possible, and for this purpose we are establishing a method to send them in small parcels amongst Friends all over England.... If you approve the method and think it worth while you shall have a parcel ... always sent you when I do anything I think worth your while." Fransham did approve and began to get and hand out parcels often. "I am glad you receiv'd the several parcels," Defoe wrote him later, "but I hear not whether 100 Reviews sent you every time since according to your order came to hand."[19] The question earlier, of course, was not "Is there evidence pamphlets and papers got into the countryside?" but "How many constituencies could each published piece reach?" The answer is that we do not know.

A third question, no easier to answer than the others: How many constituencies had enough literate electors to make propaganda worthwhile? Other students of this period have pointed out that illiteracy did not necessarily prevent the dissemination of propaganda or hamper its effect. Many scholars have quoted the author of the *Rehearsal:* "the greatest part of the people do not read books; most of them cannot read at all; but they will gather together about one that can read, and listen to an *Observator* or *Review*, as I have seen them, in the streets."[20] There are many references to the careful attention given anything printed in that period. Papers were not simply read and discarded, but went from hand to hand, not only in coffeehouses and pubs which frequently took them to draw customers, but

19. Fr. Norgate, ed., "Correspondence between Defoe and John Fransham of Norwich (1704–1707)," pp. 260–263.

20. Cranfield, p. 189.

in market places, at race meetings, and in quarter sessions of justices of the peace.[21]

But we cannot gainsay the importance of a literate electorate if propaganda is to have an impact. On the matter of literacy itself, let alone literacy among electors, authorities disagree because of the dearth of information.[22] One says, "the state of eighteenth century education was hardly sufficient in itself to create a reading public." Another disagrees, pointing out the work in primary education of the Society for Promoting Christian Knowledge and the Charity Schools movement, and calling attention to the existence of numerous town and village schools. No one can produce the necessary figures, however, which does not help much in our quest for literate electors. But we shall guess, just as they did, after looking briefly at some aspects of the electoral system which seem relevant to the question we are trying to answer.

Trying to write anything about the constituencies which sent members to Westminster would be maddening but for the excellent work already done by Robert Walcott.[23] Some of his remarks about the types and sizes of parliamentary franchises seem pertinent to the question about literate electorates. Two constituencies, the Universities of Oxford and Cambridge, certainly had literate electors. The forty county electorates are a little more difficult to take for granted. They were large—their average size being around four thousand—and potentially worth a propaganda campaign. Voters were forty-shilling free-

---

21. Ibid., pp. 187–189.
22. See ibid., pp. 185–187.
23. *English Politics*, chap. 2, "The Electoral System in 1701." See also J. H. Plumb, "The Growth of the Electorate in England from 1600 to 1715," pp. 90–116, and the relevant chapters in Holmes, *British Politics*.

holders or better, which meant that they included men of wealth and education as well as those with little of either. But probably the majority of them, rich and not so rich, could at least read and write. They were the ones who had studied at schools in village or town, if not with tutors and at the universities. And so we have forty-two constituencies sending eighty-four members who were potential targets for propaganda.

But there were others among the boroughs. Even if we dismiss many of the 203 boroughs because of their size (more than 40 percent had less than 100 voters) or their domination by some interest, we still have a significant number of relatively large, independent boroughs which probably had numbers of literate electors. The twenty or so large and medium-sized scot-and-lot boroughs with electorates of local taxpayers were likely to contain a certain number of readers. Walcott says these were perhaps "the most independent and least venal of all the boroughs."[24]

Then there were the so-called freeman boroughs whose voters had been admitted by the guilds or governing bodies to the "freedom" of the borough. Nine medium-sized and nineteen large freeman electorates were fairly independent and also, because of their large trading and commercial elements, potential readers of propaganda. Defoe's agent in Norwich, which was one of the large freeman constituencies, did comment on how "few there are amongst Tradesmen of which our City chiefly consists that set any great value upon Books," but he had been trying to get them to subscribe for publication of Defoe's *Jure Divino*, a long philosophic poem on the evils of divine right monarchy—a subject most readers would not care to explore in depth. He remarked that many tradesmen had

24. *English Politics*, p. 13.

previously subscribed for books, never to see them published, and had made up their minds not to be taken in again. Furthermore "the greatest part of this City would have subscribed for the contrary subject," so he thought he had done well to get the list he had.[25] Of course party writings were briefer than the average treatise, cheap, and fired by animus, and would therefore have readers who scarcely read anything else. Be that as it may, if we total all the boroughs where propaganda might be read, we have between forty-five and fifty. Added to the universities and counties we have constituencies which returned 175 to 180 members, if we consider only those large enough to have had potential audiences. Even a much smaller number than this would have been worth the efforts of propagandists. Changes in fewer constituencies could change the temper of Commons and signify altogether different fortunes for party leaders in intraparliamentary struggles.

There is a last question before we go to the audience toward which propaganda was aimed. Did partisan writings mold thinking on issues or simply reflect what the politically conscious were thinking? Drawing too arbitrary a distinction between these two functions is not our intention and probably is not possible. After all, partisan literature may not only embody existing feelings and thoughts about issues but solidify or otherwise change them. Existing feelings and thoughts become less inchoate, more articulate, and are thus more than reflected in political literature. The general molding influence of propaganda on the short-lived issues seems obvious. Because news was hard to get voters did not know much about those issues except what they read. What they read did shape their opinion

---

25. Norgate, "Correspondence between Defoe and John Fransham," pp. 260–263.

of, for instance, the tack controversy of 1705, the Pretender's invasion of 1708, or the Sacheverell case of 1710, and the relevance of these issues to the mainstreams of Toryism and Whiggism. Similarly the War of the Spanish Succession, one of the permanent issues of the period, would be protean enough, given the changing fortunes of war, that new information and interpretations of its partisan implications might attract attention, begin reflection, and perhaps influence thinking. But the permanent issues by way of contrast were familiar, so familiar that often the politically conscious would likely be more confirmed in their convictions and biases than moved to new attitudes by anything written on the safety of the church or the revolution settlement. This propaganda seemed aimed primarily at hardening the will of the faithful and rallying wavering or nominal supporters; the devices were predictable, few, and simple, the style not particularly varied or original. Such propaganda is important, nonetheless, because it is the touchstone of party distinctions and one very important means by which those distinctions continued through the reign of Queen Anne.

For whom would election propaganda be written and why for them? Churchmen obviously were one element of opinion. Literate and passionately interested in politics, they were avid readers and occasionally themselves writers of propaganda. But the gentry and merchants were even more significant numerically and electorally. Possessing both the ability and leisure to read, they no less than churchmen were the reason for the quantities of propaganda which poured off the presses. They were generally independent in an age when corruption and political influence were growing steadily, and since many of them were freeholders they constituted a great uncertain factor in those elections not controlled by patronage.

The gentry were particularly strong in the counties and were often able to carry elections by sheer weight of numbers. When elected themselves these men took their responsibilities seriously and zealously guarded the interests of their county and country. During the early years of the eighteenth century nearly two hundred of them sat in any given House of Commons, and their presence gave a peculiar twist to national politics.[26] Heavily Tory, they were seldom united enough to pursue a definite policy in Parliament, but they constituted a great balance that could act decisively in a conflict between organized groups. They also exerted their force by occasionally initiating and more often by supporting programs for parliamentary reform, removal of abuses in the electoral system, purity of elections, and safeguarding the position of the church.

The obstinate independence of the gentry was given a sharp edge by adverse economic conditions. Their income came mainly from the land, and they were plagued during the period by bad harvests which culminated in a real agricultural crisis in 1708–1709.[27] Lord Stanhope of Shelford wrote to his cousin James Stanhope just a month before the new reign began, "my Tenants never paid my rents so ill as this last half year which puts me in a streight for money to pay off my tradesmen in this little dirty town." A month later he told his cousin, "I have sent an attorney among my tenants to force them to pay me my rents, but he finds that all their corn lyes dead upon their hands so that to seize their persons when they have no money among them will do no good."[28] It is small wonder that the lesser and middling gentry, bowed down by mortgages and debts, should

26. J. H. Plumb, *Sir Robert Walpole: The Making of a Statesman* (1956), p. 65. See pp. 14–29 for a masterly account of the gentry and merchants.

27. Mary Ransome, "Church and Dissent in the Election of 1710," p. 89.

28. Plumb, *Walpole*, p. 16.

view darkly the heavy burden of taxation necessitated by the long wars of William's and Anne's reigns. Nor is it surprising that they should come to envy and hate the rich merchants and noblemen who in their eyes daily grew more prosperous at the nation's and their expense. Many of them were like Sir Thomas Cave of Leicestershire who fiercely hated taxes, Dutchmen, placemen, courtiers, and London moneylenders and who got himself elected to Parliament to combat these evils.[29]

The merchants in the boroughs were no less independent than the gentry. These men were always disposed to listen to any propaganda with a strong moralist bias, for they themselves were strongly attracted to the puritanical outlook with its emphasis on hard work, thrift, and plain living. Especially attractive to them was that general Protestant doctrine of individual judgment—it accorded well with their own firm independence. They were perhaps even less predictable in their political views than the gentry, for they had not the unity or self-consciousness of that class, and it was much more difficult to anticipate their reaction to any but the broadest issues. As a rule they were anxious to maintain the status quo, driven by the caution that great wealth and power produce in those possessing them. Generally Whig in their politics, they could adopt a quasi-Toryism if occasion demanded. Above all they wanted the peace and security so necessary if their commercial empires were to thrive and grow. But some of them chafed at the restraints of a static society. They were happy with the long wars with France and incensed by the Peace of Utrecht because it ended those splendid opportunities for self-aggrandizement afforded by the war effort.

At the turn of the century the merchants were a weighty in-

---

29. Margaret Lady Verney, ed., *Verney Letters of the Eighteenth Century* (1930), I, 214–256.

fluence in most of the larger boroughs—a natural concomitant to the rapid rise in their numbers and wealth throughout the seventeenth century; and although they generally looked to the government (a Whig one preferably) to provide security and stability for their business activities, they brooked no interference in the affairs of these boroughs. By weight of numbers and economic power they dominated London and heavily influenced its political complexion.[30] But it was no oligarchical domination, for they were not a homogeneous class and London was not to be controlled by either the government or its leading citizens. In the commercial cities of the provinces their presence produced similar conditions. Bristol, prosperous and flourishing, was dominated by tobacco and sugar magnates and slave traders who frequently sat in Parliament for their borough. The electorate was large, so coercion or bribery could not be effective. It was simply a logical arrangement that the town's leading citizens should be elected, particularly if, like Edward Colston, they had been so fortunate as to make a name and another fortune in London also. As was usual in such a constituency those great merchants and local landlords who attempted to influence elections counterbalanced one another, leaving the electors ample room for free choice.[31] Hull was another thriving city, also dominated by merchants of long standing, Baltic and Dutch traders. Here again the electorate was large, and elections were contested frequently and fiercely by local candidates. Although the powerful trading families had a preponderant voice in nominating candidates, the large constituency made its own choice.[32]

30. Plumb, *Walpole*, pp. 50–54.

31. Ibid., pp. 24–25, and J. H. Plumb, "Elections to the House of Commons in the Reign of William III" (Dissertation, 1939), pp. 83–84.

32. Plumb, *Walpole*, p. 25, and "Elections to the House of Commons," p. 89.

Sometimes in these boroughs control was vested in a combination of both merchants and gentry. In Exeter,[33] for example, there was a large and influential trading element which, with the less numerous but equally powerful local gentry, monopolized the control of the borough's political affairs. But in these groups there was no dominant political interest. The celebrated West Country independence appears again and again in the politics and elections of the city, and throughout the late seventeenth and early eighteenth centuries both Whigs and Tories represented Exeter in Parliament.

Finally there were the clergy, perhaps the most predictable of the three elements of early eighteenth-century public opinion. They were split over issues which had grown out of the revolution of 1688, dividing themselves into so-called High Churchmen and Low Churchmen according to their belief or disbelief in royal supremacy in religious affairs, divine hereditary-right monarchy, and passive obedience.[34] Not only was the split ideological but also hierarchic, since High Churchmen predominated among the lower clergy and Low Churchmen among the upper. But within these two camps there was considerable agreement about most political issues, particularly those pertaining to the revolution of 1688. Perhaps because most political thinking of the period did focus on the revolution of 1688 the clergy took an active interest in politics. As preachers, pamphleteers, and political organizers they did yeoman work for leaders and principles they thought vital to the church's interest.

Bishops had natural advantages as political agents. Political

---

33. For Exeter see Plumb, "Elections to the House of Commons," pp. 96–100.

34. See Norman Sykes, *Church and State in England in the Eighteenth Century* (1934); George Every, *The High Church Party* (1956); A. T. Hart, *The Country Priest in English History* (1959); A. T. Hart, *The Eighteenth Century Country Parson* (1955).

sermons were the tradition on certain anniversaries, e.g., Charles I's execution and Charles II's restoration, and on election eve; and bishops commanded larger audiences than the lesser clergy. They also held commanding positions among the large electorates of the cathedral cities even if they controlled no parliamentary seats. By verbal instructions and letters to their clergy they had much to say about the outcome of the election contests and few of them failed to use their political weight. In fact, during the reign of Anne, Lloyd of Worcester and Nicolson of Carlisle were censured by the House of Commons for overstepping what were considered normal efforts to influence the course of elections by openly canvassing their clergy against certain candidates.[35]

The lesser clergy made up in numbers for any political handicap caused by their low station in the church hierarchy. Local clergy could not always command the audiences enjoyed by prelates, but they too used the occasions for political sermons to harangue the gentry and freeholders of the shires and small county towns. Quite often they, like bishops, printed their sermons in pamphlets or wrote other treatises to propagate High Tory views. Characteristic of these pamphlets, though not the most famous of them, was Henry Sacheverell's *Discourse Showing the Dependence of Government Upon Religion* (1702). Sacheverell, destined to achieve notoriety in 1709, spoke for many of the lesser clergy when he insisted in his pamphlet that toleration should be revoked and that the church should be made an exclusive state church. The safety of the state and the constitution itself, he argued, depended on the

35. For examples of the electoral efforts of Lloyd and Nicolson see A. T. Hart, *William Lloyd, 1627–1717: Bishop, Politician, Author, and Prophet* (1952), pp. 157–160, and Francis G. James, *North Country Bishop: A Biography of William Nicolson* (1956), pp. 198–203.

safety of the church. "One cannot Flourish whilst the Other is in Distress. A Ruin'd Church and a Prosperous Government are Irreconcilable." The church was threatened by republican Whigs who under the guise of moderation and protected by the practice of occasional conformity were moving to destroy it. "We must watch against these crafty, faithless, and insidious persons, who can *creep* to our altars, and partake of our sacraments, that they may be *qualified* more secretly and powerfully to undermine us." Those who wished the welfare of the church, he continued, "ought to hang out the *bloody* flag and *banner* of defiance" against the Whigs and their allies, the schismatic and potentially rebellious dissenters. "Let us steadily adhere to the good old staunch principles of our Church," he concluded, and the forces of evil would not prevail against it or the state.

Since they had ready access to the gentry and freeholders and some measure of respect because of their learning, small though it actually was, vicars had plenty of opportunities as organizers. A Whig writer remarked rather testily that the Tories bought "libels by dozens," and dispersed them among the country clergy: "I have been told they have bundled 'em up with *Briefs* and Fast-Prayers, and distributed 'em by Apparators *gratis* to the poorer Vicars and Curates."[36] At election times clergymen frequently canvassed openly for local Tory candidates. In the general election of 1710 Bishop Burnet angrily noted that churchmen "went from house to house, pressing their people to show, on this great occasion, their zeal for the Church, and now or never to save it."[37] In addition, churchmen themselves polled in large numbers for Tory candidates, particularly during the heated election contests of 1705 and 1710. In Northampton in 1710 the Tories lost only after the local clergy had

36. Cook, "Audience of Swift's Tory Tracts," p. 39.
37. *History of My Own Time* (1823), VI, 16.

half-filled the poll booth, "though several of them had no votes," and had intimidated the electors who attempted to vote for the opposition.[38] In Southampton better results attended their efforts. The clergy and staunch churchmen of the county united behind the Tory candidates and succeeded in defeating the Whig Marquis of Winchester, despite the strength of his family interest in the county. During the polling in Bristol a band of clergy headed by their dean appeared to vote for the Tories.[39]

iii

The chief issues over which the men of the early eighteenth century divided so readily did not spring forth full blown in that period: rather they matured throughout the second half of the seventeenth century, and the seeds were planted earlier. Nor was party activity a product only of the early eighteenth century. It also stretched back at least twenty-five years. It was during the Exclusion Crisis of 1679–1681 that many of the issues so important in Anne's reign were first clearly outlined within the framework of party activity. The exclusion conflict echoed many of the constitutional issues of the Civil War and anticipated many of the problems encountered during the revolution of 1688, which was itself the immediate source of most of the political and religious controversy of the early eighteenth century.

The exclusion controversy[40] centered on one important ques-

38. Mary Ransome, "The General Election of 1710" (Master's thesis, 1938), p. 68 (quoting from the *Flying Post*, November 4, 1710).

39. Ibid.

40. For the issues debated during the Exclusion Crisis I have relied heavily on O. W. Furley, "The Whig Exclusionists: Pamphlet Literature in the Exclusion Campaign, 1679–1681," pp. 19–36, and J. R. Jones, *The First Whigs: The Politics of the Exclusion Crisis, 1679–1683* (1961).

tion, whether James, Duke of York, should be barred from the succession to the throne because of his Catholic religion. In 1679 with the Popish Plot and the menace of Catholic France in the background the religious issue at stake seemed momentous, for the current belief was that Catholicism and absolutism went hand in hand. The Whigs certainly felt that way: that James would dispense with Parliament and depend solely on the French king and the pope for support. They wanted him excluded from the succession. Their justification was the contract theory—that men possessed a basic right to protect their lives and liberties, a right antedating all governments. To effect the exclusion they relied on Parliament to alter the succession as it had done many times in the past. Whigs also tried to popularize the idea that many of the Anglican clergy were papists or popishly inclined, signaling the beginning of a campaign against High Churchmen which lasted through Anne's reign.

The Tories in 1681 had little to say to the charge that the introduction of popery posed serious dangers to state and church. They did not tamely submit however. They wanted to enhance the aura of kingship and to marshal reverence for monarchy against exclusion. So their tack was that exclusion was sinful and subversive. Monarchy was instituted by God and, being divinely sanctioned, should not be resisted or disobeyed. Even an unjust or tyrannical ruler could not be lawfully resisted: such a ruler should be regarded as a judgment of God on His people. "Lawful resistance" meant "lawful deposition," and the Whigs were republicans striving "to make '81 outdo '41," regicides and Levelers who would "level each degree."[41] Succession was by divine right and could not be

41. Furley, p. 31.

altered. There was to be, as events proved, no resistance; the exclusion movement failed in 1681. After its failure the Whigs could not stiffen themselves against James's mounting the throne, despite their vehement threats to expel a popish king. Among other things the memory of 1641 was still too vivid.

The revolution of 1688, however, in the words of one scholar, "justified the policy of Exclusion."[42] James's actions proved that the crown had to be stripped formally of its dangerous prerogative powers. When the revolution came it was supported by all the important elements in the nation. What followed was anything but what the Whigs and Tories expected. The bases of the revolution were clearly Whig, not Tory, principles, but William III, the "saviour" of the "ancient constitution," refused to subject himself to any party and relied heavily on Tories who had served Charles II and James II, such as the Earl of Danby. Certain Whigs known as the Junto did make themselves indispensable enough to William to get control of the government in 1694, but a general lassitude marked party politics of the first half of William's reign, perhaps because of William's political eclecticism.[43]

What fired party activity in the last years of William's reign was the birth of a new Toryism in the "New Country Party."[44] In the years since the revolution the thinking of many Tories had undergone a subtle transformation. They learned to live with the revolution settlement and even to support it with varying degrees of enthusiasm. They began to adopt many of the devices the Whigs had employed in opposing Charles II and James II, such popular measures as the exclusion of pensioners

42. Jones, p. 217.

43. See Feiling, pp. 275–306.

44. On the rise of the New Country Party see Walcott, *English Politics*, pp. 86–87.

and placemen from Commons, opposition to a standing army and entanglement in Continental affairs. They were also chiefly responsible for passing the act establishing the Protestant succession in the Hanoverian line.[45] The line adopted by the resurgent Tories reflects the growing political influence of Robert Harley, who set out to capture the independent country squires in Parliament and throughout the country. These men had been disillusioned by the failure of the Glorious Revolution to end such hated practices as standing armies and placemen in Commons. They had usually considered themselves Whigs. Harley attempted to show them that Whig leaders had deserted them to serve William and that there was room for them in the new Tory party. His efforts were successful to a limited degree, but more important for the strength of the party was the understanding which brought various Tory leaders and their associates to enter the new combination.[46]

The reorganized Tories soon faced their first real crisis, for early in 1696 the revelation of a plot to assassinate the king precipitated Whiggish sentiments throughout the country.[47] Whig Junto leaders, sensing the political capital to be made of the plot, proposed a form of association which pronounced William the "rightful and lawful King of these realms" and vowed to avenge his death should he be assassinated. The Tories, suddenly faced once again with the same dilemma they had encountered in 1688, became thoroughly disorganized: many of them, including several prominent New Country leaders, felt that they could not in conscience subscribe to the association. The jubilant Whigs, eager to confound the Tory

45. Ibid., pp. 87–89, and David Ogg, *England in the Reigns of James II and William III* (1955), pp. 474–476.

46. See Harley's correspondence with these Tories in H.M.C., Portland MSS, III, 351–625, passim.

47. See Feiling, pp. 318–320 for a fuller discussion of these events.

conscience, hurried through Parliament a bill which stipulated that all office and place holders as well as future members of Parliament must sign the association. The Tory gloom thickened, but Harley's counsel was to subscribe, even at the expense of violating deeply held convictions, for the greater question at stake was the future of the party.[48] His advice prevailed, and many Tories signed the association.

Then it was the Whigs' turn to be nonplussed. The sudden revelation in late 1696 that some of their highest leaders had been engaged in treasonable correspondence with James II horrified the majority of Whigs and left them shaken, just as the Tories had been earlier. The New Country party attacked. They led Commons to request that William reduce the size of his army. After the general election of 1698 the tide of opinion had swung so heavily against the Whigs that the Tories who had campaigned successfully against courtiers, placemen, taxes, and standing armies resolved to demonstrate that government without their cooperation was impossible. They completely disrupted the transaction of governmental affairs. Nothing served them so well as the Partition Treaties of 1698 and 1699. The treaties, arising from the desire of William and Louis XIV to avoid a war over the disposition of the Spanish inheritance, were not in themselves objectionable to the Tories because the instruments had already been superseded by the publication of the will of Charles of Spain and its general acceptance in Europe. What the Tories screamed about was the allegedly unconstitutional way in which Somers, the lord keeper and a Junto Whig, had put the Great Seal to a blank commission for the first Partition Treaty. In the melee which followed they impeached not only Somers but also two other Junto Whig

48. H.M.C., Portland MSS, III, 575: Robert Harley to William Bromley, April 28, 1696.

ministers, Orford and Halifax, for peculation. Only the dissolution of Parliament and a temporary resurgence of the Whigs because of the war clouds gathering over Europe ended the Tory attacks.[49] But the issue was not closed: the Tories would reopen it at the earliest opportunity, and in 1702 this did not seem to them to be far away. Surely the new queen would support them. But this was not enough. It was essential that control of Parliament be won in the first general election of the new reign.

---

49. See Feiling, pp. 322–359, for a fuller narrative. The summoning of convocation in 1701 also inflamed the last year of William III's reign, more than any other event, according to G. S. Holmes and W. A. Speck, eds., *The Divided Society: Parties and Politics in England, 1694–1716* (1968), pp. 49–50.

The General Election of 1702

I There are a number of indications that politicians of all hues regarded the election of 1702 as significant. Many Tories seemed to think the queen's accession heralded a crusade against irreligious republican Whigs. The new queen herself had lent sanction to this mood by an early public speech: "my own principles must always keep me entirely firm to the Interests and Religion of the Church of England and will incline me to countenance those who have the truest zeal to support it."[1] Some Whigs, on the other hand, feeling themselves under a pall of royal displeasure and far from hopeful about their political prospects, felt a compulsion to see that as many of their own sort as possible should be sent to Westminster to prepare against anything the Tories might attempt. Such feelings would seem to presage a bitter and busy battle in print. But judging from what was actually written, it would appear that only a few politicians really thought of the press as an electoral device yet. There was only one markedly partisan journal, the *Observator*, and the pamphlets and other pieces were not numerous. Partisan rancor was high in what was published, but the quantity and quality of what was published was inferior to that of most subsequent elections. So if the ideological side of party was important in the election of 1702, it was as much in the exploration of the use of party propaganda, in reaffirming the traditional principles of Toryism and Whiggism and in establishing touchstones for future ideo-

1. *Journals of the House of Lords, 1578–1714* (1846), XVII, 150.

logical struggles as in winning certain kinds of voters in the counties and larger boroughs.

The touchstone of Toryism since the Exclusion Crisis had been the safety of the church. Under William III many churchmen, especially those known as High Churchmen, High Tories, or sometimes Highflyers, had agonized over what was happening to the church with William's appointment of Low Churchmen or latitudinarians to the episcopacy and his own obvious lip-serving conformity.[2] Tories grumbled and waited for happier times with the accession of Anne. When that time came in March, 1702, they expected to revoke the grant of toleration and make the church once again an exclusive state church. Among their number they reckoned two members of the queen's new administration, Laurence Hyde, the Earl of Rochester, and Daniel Finch, the Earl of Nottingham, both of whom were known for their zealous churchmanship.[3] Rochester did cause tongue-clucking among churchmen occasionally for his intemperance, but he clung steadfastly to true church principles. It would not be surprising to discover that these two were responsible for the propaganda focusing on the safety of the church. Nottingham in his new position as secretary of state for the southern department certainly had natural advantages for propaganda production if he wanted to use them; Henry St. John, Viscount Bolingbroke, used the same position to sponsor the *Examiner* in 1710 and manage a coterie of writers.

Whatever the hand of Nottingham or Rochester in the mat-

2. Gareth V. Bennett, "King William III and the Episcopate," in *Essays in Modern English Church History* (1966), pp. 104–131, is the latest on William and the church and dates William's preferment of Whig Churchmen from 1694.

3. The ministerial changes on Anne's accession are discussed in Walcott, *English Politics*, pp. 97–98.

ter, James Drake wrote their sentiments and those of many other Tories in *Some Necessary Considerations Relating to all Future Elections of Members to Serve in Parliament, Humbly Offer'd to all Electors.*[4] Drake called on all men to rally to the support of the queen and the church: "Reason and Experience have both taught, that our Church and Constitution must of Necessity stand or fall together; and that all those, of Whatsoever Sect or Denomination, who have aim'd at the Subversion of one, have labour'd the Destruction of the other likewise." Drake left no doubt in the minds of his readers to whom he was referring. Although he did not use the name Whig, he made explicit reference to the "Men who, in a Reign preceding, had like, by their great Moderation and Temper, to have ruin'd our Religion, Laws, and Liberty." He warned the electors to beware of two types of candidates: "such as think Ecclesiastical Policy and external Forms of Worship Things indifferent ... and next, the modest Protestant Dissenters ... who, tho' dissatisfied with the Form of Worship establish'd in the Church of England, yet by their Separation, aim at nothing more than the Liberty of serving God in their own way." These men were dangerous, Drake continued, because they would remove the

4. The House of Lords prosecuted him for publishing another of his works, *The History of the Last Parliament* (1702), but he was acquitted. He was in and out of trouble with authorities over his works until his death in March, 1707, which was brought on partly by "ill usage from some of his party." What that "ill-usage" was, or Drake's ties with politicians were, if any, no one thought worth mentioning. See his life in the *Dictionary of National Biography* (1908–1909), v, 1351–1352. Drake's high churchmanship was echoed by many other writers, among them Henry Sacheverell, a Fellow of Magdalen College who enjoyed the patronage of Sir John Pakington, one of the Earl of Rochester's political allies. Sacheverell wrote *The New Association of Those Called Moderate Churchmen, with the Modern Whigs and Fanaticks to Undermine and Blow up the Present Church and Government* (1702). A similar work (but anonymously written) was *The Case Fairly Stated, in a Dialogue Between Moderation and Constitution* (1702).

church from its preeminent position and pave the way for a religious anarchy such as England witnessed in the 1640s. Let the Dissenters be satisfied with the toleration granted to them in the matter of worship, he declared, and not aspire to a voice in government, for "the History of the last threescore Years here in England sufficiently inform us how little we are to trust to the Mercy of any of our Protestant Dissenters of whatsoever Denomination, whenever in Power."

High Tories did not dominate the queen's new government; Rochester and Nottingham did not hold the highest positions. Control of the armed services, foreign relations, and the Treasury were reserved for the Marlboroughs and Sidney Godolphin, who were not staunch Tories. Two other positions went to New Country party allies of Rochester and Nottingham, Robert Harley and Sir Simon Harcourt; Harley winning speaker of Commons and Harcourt, solicitor general.[5] But whatever Tory complexion the administration might have it was by no means Whig-tinctured. Whig leaders such as the five Junto lords—Somers, Halifax, Wharton, Orford, and Sunderland—and the Duke of Newcastle were officeless as the election approached. Were they for that reason supinely accepting whatever charges the Tories cast at them? Linking any Whig leader to Whig propaganda in 1702 is extremely tenuous at best. Put bluntly, the truth is that we cannot find any Whig leader paying or issuing directives to John Tutchin, the first editor of the *Observator*, or any other Whig writers. The Earl of Halifax did show on several occasions that he thought propaganda worth a politician's time and money but he may not have stirred himself in 1702.[6] If so and Tutchin and his fel-

5. Walcott, *English Politics*, pp. 97–98.

6. In 1704, for instance, he requested that Charles Davenant, who by then had had a change of heart and employment, do a tract on the need for unity to

low Whig writers were working gratis, or just for what they could get by selling their papers, the Junto and other Whig leaders were getting something for nothing because Tutchin and other writers who took up the issue of the church's safety tried to ward off Tory assaults on Whig churchmanship.

In the *Observator*[7] and various pamphlets, along with the usual fulminations against High Churchmen and their popish tendencies, the Whigs also included indictments of their conduct in earlier reigns. Under James II, they charged, High Churchmen surrendered the charters of liberties into the hands of a popish government and persuaded the king that he might *jure divino* take away the estates and lives of their fellow countrymen. These men ought to be opposed in the elections as "Enemies to your Country, and Friends to Popery, notwithstanding their specious Pretensions to the Church of England."[8] High Churchmen, another writer warned, only adopt the cause of the church to ingratiate themselves with the people; their true aims are "caressing, herding with, defending and courting of nonjurors, Papists and Jacobites ... which show how far they love the Protestant Religion, Religion established in the Church."[9]

---

carry on the war. See Davenant's biography in the *Dictionary of National Biography*, v, 549–550. And in 1713 he spent money on the *British Merchant*, a Whig paper. See Hanson, *Government and the Press*, p. 105.

7. John Tutchin aided by John Howe began the paper on April 1, 1702, as a biweekly, editing it until his death in September, 1707, which occurred following a beating by men who did not like his views. The paper continued after a pause under other hands but still with decidedly Whig views, even (in 1708) strong Whig Junto views. Tutchin got into trouble often; in 1704, for instance, he displeased and had to stand trial before the House of Commons. See Stevens, *Party Politics*, pp. 10, 77.

8. *Observator*, no. 25, July 19, 1702.

9. *King William's Affection to the Church of England Examin'd* (1703). W. T. Morgan in *Bibliography of British History* says that Daniel Defoe wrote this tract. This is largely conjecture but possibly true. In any event Defoe was probably free-lancing in 1702.

In a later issue of the *Observator* the Whigs argued that the true pillars of the church were not the High Churchmen but the "moderate" clergy. They warned: "Never chuse a Man that is so high in Religion as to over-look the Liberties of the People; Extreams on either hand are very Dangerous. It is an old Proverb, *Longus homo raro Sapiens*, a tall Man is generally a Fool: It is the same thing in Opinions, the higher they are, the further distant they are from the Truth, which, as well, as Virtue, consists in a Mediocrity."[10]

This sparring over the church expanded, overlapping into a second issue, the Glorious Revolution and its attendant principles. The question of the revolution would recur in every election of the period. It was the sort of fundamental issue on which pages and pages could be written without much effort or thought—a religious fundamental—and Whig writers found the issue a good stick with which to beat Tories. The Tories, having accepted 1688 in fact if not in theory, were in a political quandary. Tory propagandists might fulminate against dissenters and republicans, but their own doctrines of nonresistance, passive obedience, and hereditary right were altogether antithetical to the revolution settlement. G. M. Trevelyan has written: "This uneasiness of the Tory, and particularly of the clerical, conscience, and the uncertain and wavering character of Tory sympathies in relation to the exiled James and his son and grandson, constitute a fact of great historical importance. ... The Revolution had made the Tories ... for two generations to come, a party with a poor logical position and an uneasy mind, often divided into opposite camps at a crisis."[11]

10. *Observator*, no. 27, July 25, 1702.

11. G. M. Trevelyan, *The English Revolution, 1688–1689* (1938), pp. 148–149.

Tory political philosophy was in fact moribund, as the events of 1714–1715 were to show.

Whig writers naturally exploited the Tory dilemma, then, without need for encouragement from political leaders, as they would in succeeding elections. They asserted that Tory principles were conducive to a tyranny in which the monarch, emboldened by such principles, would ruthlessly stamp out individual liberties. The Whigs obviously could not go so far as to say that Queen Anne would ever become such a ruler, but they could and did allude to the Pretender. They charged that the Tory defense of hereditary and divine right were calculated to sow doubt in the minds of Anne's loyal subjects, since emphasizing these principles could lead only to a restoration of the Pretender. The queen's title, they maintained, while not dependent solely on parliamentary sanction derived much of its strength from that fact. To declare otherwise was tantamount to encouraging the pretensions of the "prince" beyond the waters. As one Whig writer put it in the *Observator*,[12] the Tories endeavor "to Un-Queen her, by insinuating that Her Majesty has only a Right by Succession. . . . [They] talk very oddly about Her most Gracious Majesties Right to the Crown: I protest I don't know what to think of them, they can mean nothing but rebellion by what they say."

Several Tory writers seemed to feel that some reply to these charges was necessary, but they offered no single answer, which may imply that, like the Whigs, they got no direction from higher-ups about exactly what to say. Would Whig propaganda have stung Nottingham and Rochester? Probably so given

12. *Observator*, no. 28, July 29, 1702. See also *A New Test of the Church of England's Loyalty: Or Whiggish Loyalty and Church Loyalty Compared* (1702).

their staunch commitment to High Churchism. They would not have had to commission specific replies, however, since these would have been part of the same fundamentalism which prompted the Whig attacks. The replies became stock for Tory pamphleteers in succeeding elections. Denying that passive obedience, nonresistance, and divine right monarchy were vital points of Tory doctrine was one answer.[13] Aspersing the Whigs for raising such distasteful matters under so glorious and merciful a queen as Anne was another. One anonymous writer assailed the Whigs for lese majesty, declaring that they were traducing the queen by insisting on her parliamentary right to the throne. If she depends on the people for her title, he went on, then the "Brainless Crowd" make the ruler, "as Potters do their Vessels, and . . . they have Power to crush them in pieces whenever they do not like them."[14] Whoever he was, the writer had a point, but that was the best he or any Tory could do. They evaded the issue generally unless there was some specific cause they could attach it to, as in 1705 and 1710, and understandably so, since they had no viable doctrine to oppose to Whig principles. The revolution had cut the taproot of the Tory creed. It was subsisting in large measure on reserve stores of sentimentality and nostalgia. Many Tories undoubtedly saw the handwriting on the wall, and for them the Tory creed was only a sentimental pose that could be easily discarded in 1714. But their more conscientious (or perhaps doctrinaire) brethren would carry the accursed albatross of Tory political philosophy firmly fastened about their necks until late in the century when there would arise a new Toryism owing little more than its name to the Toryism of the early eighteenth century.

---

13. *The Case Fairly Stated.*

14. *The Observator Observ'd: or; a Scourge for an Ingrateful Rebel to Flaug him thro' London Instead of Devonshire* (1702).

Much different in character was the third issue: William III's last Whig-dominated ministry and its policies was different from the two other issues in its recency and concreteness, qualities which argue for its deliberate creation by members of the new administration. But this issue, if indeed it was raised by certain Tory leaders, could not have been to the liking of all the new government. Marlborough and Godolphin had no reason to love the Junto Whigs. However they did believe in the Junto's foreign policy, the Continental land campaigns against Louis XIV, and they had nothing to gain by attacking potential allies for coming votes on war supplies.[15] Rochester, on the other hand, loved neither the Junto nor its idea of engaging the French in the Netherlands. If there must be war he was for a "blue water" policy of purely naval warfare, the policy advocated later by William Pitt the Elder, and made no secret of his views. He opposed Marlborough's intention to fight in the Netherlands and by his obstinacy actually slowed up the declaration of war for two months after Anne's accession. War declared, Rochester's obstreperousness did not cease and he eventually wore out the patience of Godolphin and Marlborough. But for the summer of 1702 he had clearly and publicly divorced himself from the administration's war policy which picked up where William and the Whigs had left off.[16]

Rochester had reason to raise questions about the late Whig ministers. Did his New Country party allies, Nottingham and Harley, who had pushed the Junto hard in the last months of William's reign? We do not know, but circumstantial evidence points that way. Someone who knew what he was doing wrote

15. See Holmes's discussion of Whig support for Marlborough's strategy in *British Politics*, pp. 71–72ff. Marlborough recognized how little sympathy he could expect from High Tories and resolved in May, 1702, not to let them near departments responsible for executing war policy (Holmes, p. 375).

16. Holmes, pp. 72–73.

England's Corruptions and Mismanagements Discovered in a Dialogue between Trueman and Legion, charging the Whigs (under the name of Legion) with responsibility for corruption in the navy, the customs, and the Post Office.[17] The pamphlet's particular concern, however, was maladministration and peculation by the admiralty and the navy commissioners. Whigs had been responsible and were anxious to go to war against France again because they had made so much from earlier wars. An enormous war debt, the writer suggested to his squirearchal and heavily taxed readers, had really lined Whig pockets. He listed figures and specifically named three Junto ex-ministers —Somers, Halifax and Orford—as he denounced "Corrupt Judges, Ministers, Publick Officers, and Magistrates" to whose fingers large sums of public money had stuck.[18] Menacing though France might be (a reader could tell that he thought the danger slight), Whig mismanagers were a greater and more immediate menace. Their removal and punishment took precedence over any other war preparations. The figures cited in the pamphlet may or may not have been accurate. What is more important for an analyst of this propaganda is that the arguments and those of other antiministerial writings read like an official line. If not inspired by some politician, it nevertheless

17. The author is anonymous but obviously knew something about finances or knew someone who did. Harley had friends on the parliamentary commission of public accounts, but so did Nottingham (Walcott, *English Politics*, pp. 100–101). In 1701 Harley had had a hand in propaganda aimed specifically at the Junto; he helped Davenant with the records in preparing *The True Picture of a Modern Whig*. A sequel to the *True Picture* appeared in the 1702 election, incidentally, entitled *Tom Double Return'd out of the Country: or the True Picture . . . in a Second Dialogue Between Mr. Whiglove and Mr. Double* (1702), attacking the Junto ministers with charges similar to the original version. This is the circumstantial evidence connecting someone from the New Country coalition with the antiadministration propaganda.

18. *A Letter to a Gentleman Elected a Knight of the Shire to Serve in the Present Parliament* (1702) singled out Orford for personal and political attacks.

became part of the Tory pamphleteer's repertoire. In 1708 and again from 1710 to 1713, when the war had lingered inconclusively for a decade at an expense that would have made the mind boggle in 1702, Tory writers would blame Whig greed and dishonesty for the war and its interminableness.

Tory writers also seem to make a concerted effort to discredit William III's foreign policy, a policy with which the Junto had become identified and which the chief ministers of Anne had adopted. The split between Rochester and his High Tory allies and Marlborough and Godolphin over war policy did not mean that the latter were attacked directly by Tory propaganda. That would have been striking too close to the throne, Anne herself having concurred in the new ministry's war aims. But the Whigs could be attacked, and the Dutch, and through them, William III. That would be accomplishing several desirable things at one stroke: discrediting the Whigs, exploiting a latent public anti-Dutch bias and the country's coolness toward the late king, urging a "blue water" policy and bringing pressure to bear on Marlborough and Godolphin.

Charles Davenant's *Tom Double Return'd Out of the Country* charged that the Whigs' aim had been to make England a Dutch dependency and a tool to carry out Dutch policies on the Continent and declared that England's true interests lay seaward.[19] That was putting it a bit strongly and the House of Lords condemned the pamphlet. But another writer asked

19. Davenant, as notes 6 and 17 above indicate, first got himself recognition in Tory circles by his attacks on Whig ministers. In 1699 he did a tract, *Discourse of Grants and Resumptions*, against Somers, Halifax, and others who had, it insisted, pillaged royal Irish revenues for themselves. He had reasons for his rancor in addition to principle because he had not been continued in a post as commissioner of the excise by William III. Soon after the election of 1702 he ended his partisan work for the High Tories, and by 1704 was urging unity to carry on the war.

whether "England ought to contribute as much to the support of the Confederacy, as the Dutch, whose Countreys are contigious to the Enemies Territories, and therefore in more Danger . . . ?"[20] *The Miseries of England, From the Growing Power of her Domestick Enemies* expressed similar doubts: "why should we that have least cause to fear, Defend a Neighbour whom the Danger's near, And we endure the Toil, and pay the Cost, When they, without our Help, must needs be lost."

Since Tory writers had named the Junto leaders specifically, it is difficult to think that they did not wish to respond. And whether put up to it by the Junto or not, some Whig writers went at the Tories with a will, charging them with treason and Jacobitism and defending the policy of striking at France through the Netherlands. One anonymous writer said that there was a "French faction" working to hand England over to the French king. It had opposed all William's war measures and was still trying to keep the country from prosecuting the war.[21] The "depressing of Holland and exalting of France" signified Jacobitism to another writer. He thought all the talk about letting the Dutch fight their own wars proved that there was a plot to bring in the Pretender and enslave England to

20. *A Speech Without Doors, Concerning the Most Effectual Way of Providing Forty Thousand Landsmen, as England's Quota in the Present Grand Confederacy* (1702). See also James Drake, *History of the Last Parliament*, which not only puts forth similar views but, because Drake wrote it, constitutes a reason for linking High Tory Church and war strategy propaganda. Views similar to *A Speech Without Doors* were also in *The Modern Whig Dictator: or, the Exultation: a Satyr* (1702).

21. *Division our Destruction: or, a Short History of the French Faction in England* (1702). See also *The Moderator, or a View of the State of the Controversy Betwixt Whigg and Tory* (1702) and the *Observator*, no. 30, August 5, 1702.

France and Rome.[22] This was only riposting Tory charges of corruption and mismanagement. More care was given to defending the Netherlands campaigns as sound policy. So carefully was the job done that it might have had the blessings of Anne's chief advisors rather than the Junto, if it indeed had any important political encouragement.

The *Debate Between Three Ministers of State*[23] treated the Tory views seriously as worthy of logic rather than invective. One minister, obviously representing the Tory view, opposed the war as fruitless, arguing that there would be no victor. He stressed the large debts still unpaid, the heavy casualties of the previous fighting, and the ruinous effects the war would have on commerce. Let us remain behind our sea wall, he urged. "Must we contribute the choicest Liquor of our Veins, and the best Moneys in our Pockets, to facilitate the Emperors Progress? I say no; for, there's no part to be taken in this War, which will not be destructive; so, the best will be to take no Part . . . and in the mean time, to provide for improving our Wealth at home." Another minister thought him shortsighted. "After the French have Triumphed over the Emperor, and his Allies having Spain as their Vassalage, they will be Masters over our Fortune too." This minister urged a union with the Dutch against France, with England raising both an army and a fleet for the enterprise. "Our safety," he declared, "lies in maintaining the 'Balance of Europe,'" for by "uniting with Holland, we do follow our true interest, which hath ever been successful to this Nation, which is to be still Masters at Sea, and by Embracing

22. *A Short Defence of the Last Parliament, Answer'd Article by Article* (1702).

23. The title itself makes this a curious piece. Was it an outgrowth of intraministerial squabbling between Marlborough and Rochester?

the Emperor's Interest, we may hope for a considerable Portion in the Spoils of the Spanish Indies." This anonymous minister was William III resurrected; the "Balance of Europe" had been the quest of his adult life. The Junto Whigs had joined him in it and Marlborough had taken it up. It had serious opposition among many Tories, and as Anne's reign grew longer the opposition grew. But in 1702 because the new queen had decided for the Continental land campaigns, so it would be for most Englishmen.

The probability that certain politicians wanted to argue specific issues in print seems strong, but are there signs of more encompassing interests? Asking whether there were party platforms is putting the question a bit too strongly. Put another way, were the issues argued separately or were they enmeshed in a more broadly oriented electoral appeal? In the midst of the elections the *Observator* urged voters to make careful choices, to find out before they voted for a man whether he had opposed the revolution, had been against making William and Mary king and queen, had denied their "rightful and lawful" title to the throne, and finally, whether he had refused to support William in preserving "the Balance of Europe"? If he did, reject him, the paper said. He is a man of "French Principles" who will "Traffick with your Liberties, and set even your Country to Sale."[24] Tutchin or whoever wrote the issues for him was putting the best Whig foot forward because the revolution and war strategy were issues on which the Whigs thought they looked best. James Drake did the same job for the Tories. He chose a full-length sheet of issues on which Tories had an edge, or thought they did, particularly the safety of the church and the alleged misconduct of the Junto Whig ministers, and put

24. *Observator*, nos. 25, 26, July 19, 22, 1702.

them together in an appeal to electors to choose men who "are true sons of the Church of England, as by Law Established, . . . were for the enquiring into the Misapplication and Embezzlement of forfeited Estates, and publick Money . . . have provided for the Deficiencies of the Publick Funds, and the Payment of the publick Debts, and the Preservation of Parliamentary Credit . . . [and] have shew'd an extraordinary and singular zeal and Affection for her Majesty's Person, Interest, and Government." The other particulars on the sheet read like the program the New Country coalition of Rochester, Nottingham, and Harley had pursued for the preceding half-dozen years. It was tacked on to James Drake's *Some Necessary Considerations*, a work already noted above for its High Churchmanship and High Toryism. Perhaps we should not be too easily convinced it was the work of the coalition. What is certain are the broad concerns of the pamphlet, concerns which went beyond the specific issues politicians had reasons to fight about, and which constitute a party appeal.

Not so dramatically as these examples but nonetheless clearly, most pamphlets and papers cited above also make a broadly oriented electoral appeal. Few propaganda pieces argue only one issue even though they may concentrate on a specific issue. And that raises another question. If William III's last Whig ministry and war strategy was a deliberately contrived issue, as the consistency and unity of the two sets of arguments attest, does that mean that the other issues lumped with it in the pamphlets and papers were to some measure instigated? I think it does. Not only were single issues enmeshed in a broad electoral appeal frequently, but also intertwined with each other. Preserving the "Balance of Europe" was vital to the Whigs because if France mastered Europe it would soon master England, crushing the revolution settlement and the constitution which, as they thought, had brought England out of the miasma of arbitrary government. Many Tories were worried about the constitution also, but they thought France less a menace than irreligious republican Whigs. The real enemy for them was the enemy within: fifth columnists who kept insisting on moderation in religious doctrine and the right of rebellion against unjust rulers. That kind of talk was softening the foundations of orderly government, they thought. Until it stopped and those who were doing the talking were put down, it would not make much difference what was done about the enemy outside. Now all these indications of propaganda management are really rather tenuous since we do not have the hard evidence to link politicians with even the issue of war strategy. But, taken with a measure of skepticism, what we have still seems to point toward deliberately organized, if very limited, press campaigns. These campaigns had the function of developing party positions on important issues, positions which correspond to the traditional Whiggism and Toryism and which also match in some ways with the policies and programs of the Junto Whigs and New Country (High Tory dominated) party.

The year 1702 was in effect a rehearsal for propaganda in the subsequent elections of the reign. Propaganda in elections was not a new thing, but the reign of Anne did mean a new context in which propagandists would have to learn to work. The year saw the emergence of some techniques and devices which apparently satisfied political leaders and writers and which survived through ensuing elections, techniques and devices for the most part adapted from the earlier Exclusion Crisis and the Glorious Revolution. Probably only a few writers did the work, and those few, except for John Tutchin, were of a lesser and middling sort. Tutchin would soon have the able company of Daniel Defoe, who was writing for the ministry by

1704, and Charles Leslie, who began his High Tory, High Church *Rehearsal* in 1704. They were not party hacks as their work showed. Leslie's *Rehearsal*, for instance, makes James Drake's *Some Necessary Considerations* pale in comparison. Drake was adequate; he said the right things and said them with warm conviction. But Leslie could write circles around him and he struck fire. Not only were really good writers few in 1702 but there was no one to argue for the ministry, a deficiency Robert Harley thought needed correcting before the next elections. So only a few months after the general election of 1702 Harley, who was finding it necessary to cast in with Godolphin and Marlborough if he wanted access to power and influence and to avoid the opposition into which Nottingham and Rochester were drifting, was pressing the urgent need for a government spokesman. He fixed on Defoe.[25]

What had this propaganda to do with the election contests themselves? In its immediate forms, that is in pamphlets and papers passed around or sold in specific constituencies, it seemed to have little to do with the contests of the summer of 1702. There is not a single constituency about which we have the kind of evidence we want; we know nothing about specific pamphlets or papers being used in constituencies. It seems most likely that propaganda would find readers and play a discernible part in the elections in the counties and larger freeman and scot-and-lot boroughs, and it was precisely there that ideological issues figured noticeably, if not exactly measurably, in contests.

In the county of Worcester, ideology impinged on local concerns in the personal and partisan rivalry between the two protagonists of the contest, William Lloyd, Bishop of Worcester and a leading Whig, and Sir John Packington, one of the county

25. Stevens, p. 47.

members in Parliament and a fervid Tory.[26] Their feud had begun in the reign of William III when Lloyd was translated to the diocese of Worcester. He found himself officiating over a hotbed of High Toryism led by Packington. Lloyd, a man of quick temperament, set about to vote Packington out of his seat. He tried in 1701 and failed. In view of the new queen's well-known sympathies for Tories the election of 1702 was not the time to be attempting to oust Packington, but Lloyd persisted. Soon after the Parliament rose Lloyd had had the audacity to summon Sir John and order him not to stand in the coming elections. Packington, however, knew the tenor of his constituency. He felt safe in ignoring the proud bishop and his threats to "speak against him to his clergy." True to his threats Lloyd waged a tireless campaign against his rival, ordering his clergy to vote and work against Packington if they hoped for future promotion. His own tenants he bullied and threatened, telling them that their member had "voted to bring in a French government" and that they "might as well vote for the Prince of Wales as for him." To one clergyman he wrote that Packington "was a man that strikes at the government; that he was debauched and lewd and so was his father and grandfather; that his father had filled him so full of Jacobitism, that it would not be rooted out . . . he was of the Prince of Wales' Church." Once again Lloyd wasted his efforts. Packington was returned to Parliament by a larger majority than usual. As Lloyd was to learn in succeeding elections the indomitable Worcestershire freeholders, many of whom were concealed Jacobites, were solidly behind their squire. Sir John Packington would remain a member for Worcestershire throughout Anne's

26. See Hart, *William Lloyd*, pp. 151–153, 157–162, for the Worcestershire election.

reign, surviving even the Whig triumph of 1708, and into the alien Hanoverian period.

Not only in the counties but in some of the larger boroughs as well issues and interests converged. Leicester, for example, one of the larger scot-and-lot boroughs, had a contest between a man of pronounced Toryism, Sir George Beaumont, and Lawrence Carter, the nominee of the Whig Earl of Rutland who had an interest in the county.[27] Most of the local gentry resented Rutland's choices for the county seats and the borough, Rutland apparently not being discreet or gentle enough in the machinations of his interest. But compounded with this were religious differences, at least in the minds of those who thought themselves irreproachable Tories and churchmen. The two local county candidates, John Verney and John Wilkins, feeling a need for outside influence against Rutland and what they called "presbyterianism," wrote Sir Thomas Coke of Derbyshire (who had an estate in Leicestershire) appealing for help: "Pray send to Melton [Coke's estate] to all your friends, for all the presbyterians are very busy."[28] At their request, Coke came to the pollings for whatever worth his presence might have. Obviously it helped. Rutland's men lost the county elections, and his nominee, Carter, was thrown out by Beaumont in Leicester.

These contests were not atypical, but were there enough of them to have made propaganda worthwhile? Were there enough counties and boroughs which changed hands to justify, in retrospect, an effort to argue issues? There were at least

27. See *The Victoria History of the County of Leicester* (1954), II, 122–123.

28. See Great Britain, Historical Manuscripts Commission, Report on the MSS of the Earl of Cowper, at Melbourne, III, 1–14, for all the election correspondence on which this account is based. Cited in later notes as H.M.C., Cowper MSS.

eleven counties in which changes occurred in fifteen seats; in seven of the larger boroughs there were changes in seven seats. There may have been others but these are definite. At any rate the pattern which emerges from the changes is as significant as the number of changes. Of the twenty-two changes eighteen were from Whig to Tory, either independent or associated with some group.[29] The pattern was even more overwhelming a shift than that occurring in the general election which was returning two Tories to every Whig. If the pattern holds for all the counties and larger boroughs it suggests that a good bit of the Tories' two-to-one majority was acquired in potentially issue-conscious constituencies. And if that was so, a final "if," the results were well worth the effort of arguing issues. That issues actually meant a great deal in the *winning* of these contests is the moot point. But it is important to note that contemporaries were talking about Tory victories all over the country, about the election of a "true Church of England Parliament."[30] If Tory groups and individuals were winning by a large margin across the country, they were winning by an even greater margin in "free" constituencies where influence alone could not carry the day. And that makes a rather strong argument, if a roundabout one, that ideology *was* important in the outcome of the contests.

It must be said again that while issues can be found in contests specific pieces of propaganda cannot. And if elections in these constituencies turned somewhat on issues, they were of the fundamentalist sort—the revolution settlement and the specter of Jacobitism, the safety of the church—issues with which there was already considerable familiarity and which had been

---

29. I used Walcott, *English Politics*, pp. 198–232, in analyzing these changes.

30. Feiling, *History of the Tory Party*, p. 366.

only slightly adapted to newer circumstances, and not discernibly the newer and more concrete issue of war strategy. That may indicate in its own way what many people were thinking. It was not yet clear what the war strategy of the administration meant, not even to all Tories, nor what administration policies generally meant. The queen's accession was too recent and the ministry too new. In that sense Tory propagandists really wasted their efforts attacking the Continental land campaign of the government. But they touched a vital spot with the church because the new queen had made known publicly her High Church tendencies and urged High Churchmanship. That much people did know. They could be unambiguously enthusiastic for church and queen amidst the uncertainties of the new reign.

By no stretch of the imagination was propaganda the only, or even the major, electoral effort in 1702. Not until later in the period did many politicians appreciate the pen's value, judging from the relatively small amount of material published. And so many of the election contests were influenced by local and personal interests: the relationships which politicians cultivated, and which were a staple of political life in that period. Both Whig and Tory leaders played an old electoral game which was subject to the vagaries of general political conditions. Still it was a familiar business, and much more likely to produce predictable results than any appeal to the issue-conscious in larger constituencies because the objects primarily were seats in the smaller, more numerous, and manipulatable boroughs.[31] Even brief looks at what certain leaders were able to do elec-

31. Walcott's excellent chapter on the electoral system needs citing again: *English Politics*, pp. 8–23. Electoral interests were built primarily on smaller "potwalloper" and scot-and-lot boroughs, burgage boroughs, and corporation boroughs.

torally demonstrate the importance of influence in early eighteenth-century elections and reveal the power base which made some men movers at Westminster.

Fortified by the queen's favor and offices carrying electoral influence, ministerial leaders had definite advantages and marked success. By virtue of his office as secretary of state the Earl of Nottingham was able to bring extraordinary pressure to bear on the Cinque Ports and other southern boroughs subject to government influence.[32] His friends won seven seats there, and elsewhere his allies secured seven other seats. Thus Nottingham, adding these new members to his previous ones, could boast of forty-five supporters in the first Parliament of Anne's reign. The friends of Nottingham's colleague, the Earl of Rochester, did even better in the elections.[33] Relying partly on the official influence and prestige he possessed as lord lieutenant of Ireland, and partly on the efforts of his allies, he helped return a total of sixty-six members to this Parliament, and of this total nineteen were new seats. The last important Tory leader at work in the election, Robert Harley, was not quite so successful as his colleagues but his efforts were not without some success.[34] One of his followers was elected for Cricklade against the nominee of Thomas, Lord Wharton. Harley's total number of followers in the Parliament of 1702 was twenty-one.

These victories frequently meant defeats for important Whig lords. In the last Parliament of William III the Whigs had held a decisive majority. The accession of Anne, however, had diminished their power in government and consequently their influence in the counties. They went into the elections seriously

32. For Nottingham's efforts in this election see Walcott, *English Politics*, pp. 103–104, 219–221.

33. For Rochester's efforts see ibid., pp. 104–105, 222–225.

34. Ibid., pp. 105, 225–226.

handicapped vis-à-vis their Tory opponents because of the change of administration. Even Wharton's magnificent electoral machine could not function properly in such adverse circumstances.[35] Wharton himself had suffered the full measure of Anne's displeasure: his name had been dropped from the list of privy councillors, his comptroller's staff had been taken from him in public and given on the same occasion to Seymour, and his territorial honors had been given to the Tory Lord Abingdon. In the face of such obvious royal displeasure Wharton could not hope to have the twenty-five followers he had counted in William's last Parliament. Ten of his nominees failed to be reelected in the various boroughs and counties he normally influenced. In the north, for example, Wharton's followers usually got seats at Appleby and Cockermouth where he had purchased burgages to strengthen the influence given him by large country estates. In this election Wharton's nominee for Cockermouth, Thomas Lamplugh, managed to retain his seat, but Wharton's nephew and nominee for Appleby, Wharton Dunch, failed to hold his seat, losing it to James Graham, a local Tory squire. In neighboring Yorkshire, where he had similar interests based on burgage ownership and strategically located estates, Wharton usually nominated friends for one seat at Richmond and two at Northallerton. His interest here failed him in the election of 1702. He managed to return only one candidate to Northallerton, his nominees for the other seat at the borough and at Richmond being soundly defeated by two Tories.

Wharton suffered his heaviest losses, surprisingly, in Wiltshire and Buckinghamshire where his greatest electoral influence lay. In William's last Parliament nine of Wharton's nom-

35. Ibid., pp. 39–40, 107, 229–232.

inees sat for Buckingham county and its boroughs, and four more sat for Wiltshire boroughs. In Anne's first Parliament, however, he could count on only half these supporters. Besides losing a seat at Aylesbury, normally under his control, Wharton saw his close friends lose in the elections for the county and for Buckingham, and in Wiltshire his nominees at Calne and Cricklade were also defeated.

Wharton's Junto associates,[36] Orford and Sunderland, lost about the same percentage; they would have fourteen members in this Parliament, three less than in William's last Parliament. The Earl of Halifax suffered the heaviest losses. Seven of his friends had been elected in 1701; in the elections of 1702 four of these were defeated—two of them members of his own family. Only the Earl of Somers managed to hold his own, having six supporters in the new Parliament as he had in the old.

When all the results of the first election of Anne's reign were in, it looked to many contemporaries like a Tory victory. "Many violent Whigs," Harley wrote to Godolphin, were not returned, and Tories were acclaiming the election of a "true Church of England Parliament."[37] Probably many violent Whigs had not been elected and many loyal churchmen had. Robert Walcott's data for the election add up to 321 Tories and 149 Whigs in the new Parliament.[38] There were a number of new unaligned Tories at Westminster, backbenchers of uncertain intentions except that many were loyal churchmen. What they might do toward anything except such broad measures as

36. For the activities of the other Junto Whigs see ibid., pp. 107–108, 229–232.

37. Feiling, p. 366.

38. Walcott, *English Politics*, p. 109. Walcott, of course, feels that other ways of adding the election results are as important as, if not more important than, adding up Whigs and Tories. Speck, *Tory and Whig*, p. 123, says that there were 323 Tories and 190 Whigs.

saving the church would depend on Tory leaders whose own followings were much stronger than in the old Parliament. But the victors were not agreed on what to do. Nottingham and Rochester, and probably numbers of the backbenchers, wanted one thing, while Harley, going over to the side of Marlborough and Godolphin, wanted another, and the latter ministers still another. Those divided aims and the two major issues of the next three years are really the basis for what happens until the next general election.

The General Election of 1705

II If anything argues for the importance of ideas and issues in the electoral process of the early eighteenth century it is the rapidity with which the circumstances of 1702 changed to make in 1705 one of the most ideologically rancorous and warmly contested elections of the reign.[1] Two issues, the occasional conformity crisis of 1702–1704 and the war, intertwined with the aims and actions of important leaders, were basic to producing the first emotional and turbulent election of the reign. No less essential was propaganda, not only in the election year but in the months preceding it. As party politics became more partisan that partisanship was spewed out to wider circles of people, returning to Westminster to excite further partisanship which in inflammatory print began the circuit again.

Those who considered themselves High Tories had long been troubled by the practice of occasional conformity, or the taking of the sacrament just to meet the requirements of the Corporation and Test Acts (1661 and 1673, respectively) for municipal and national office, and they had talked about doing something to end the practice in the election of 1702. Many backbenchers in the new Parliament of 1702 and the universities and clergy agreed with Dr. Henry Sacheverell that the church's supporters ought to "hang out the bloody flag and banner of defiance"

---

1. This chapter is heavily indebted to Miss Elizabeth Cunnington's unpublished Master's thesis, "The General Election of 1705," 1938. There is a rather sketchy study of the 1705 election in Morgan, *English Political Parties*, chap. 3.

against the occasional conformists.[2] The Earl of Nottingham instigated the first attack on them in November, 1702, by having a friend introduce a bill in Commons to dismiss and fine any officeholders and disfranchise any borough corporation members who took the sacrament and afterward attended a meetinghouse.[3]

As was at least partially intended, the bill had far-reaching political implications. The Whigs regarded it as a direct attack on the basis of their political power. Whig leaders in the House of Lords prevented the bill's adoption in the first session by parliamentary maneuvering, watering it down by amendments which Commons would not accept. By the beginning of the second session in the autumn of 1703 Whigs began to get support. The chief ministers and even the queen were of the opinion that the crusade against occasional conformity should be ended, that it was not worth the furor it was creating and the disruption of the government's work, notably the prosecution of the war. The question was how to do it because the issue was already a national one.[4] The queen's hinting in the opening speech that she valued union and the avoidance of "heats and divisions"[5] was one means; secret parliamentary maneuvering by the ministers was another. Pushing out of the cabinet the

2. *The Political Union, a Discourse Shewing the Dependence of Government on Religion* (1702).

3. See Holmes, *British Politics*, pp. 99–103, and Feiling, *History of the Tory Party*, pp. 360–380, on the occasional conformity crisis and its political repercussions. Nottingham had drafted a bill against occasional conformity as early as 1689: Henry Horowitz, *Revolution Politicks: The Career of Daniel Finch, Second Earl of Nottingham, 1647–1730* (1968), pp. 89–90.

4. Thomas Coke's agent in Derbyshire wrote him of the local reaction to the bill, warning that both sides were dissatisfied with his position on the matter: H.M.C., Cowper MSS, III, 20, 29–30, Michael Burton to Thomas Coke, December 28, 1702, and January, 1704.

5. William Cobbett, *Parliamentary History of England from the Norman Conquest in 1066 to the Year 1803* (1810), VI, 151, 155–158.

Earl of Rochester, who was a nuisance because of his antiwar views, was a third device. These measures stopped the bill in the second session, and envenomed feelings between supporters of the bill and its opponents. Tories were falling out with each other over the question. So serious had their differences become that Nottingham and Sir Edward Seymour, still in office and obstructionists against the war like Rochester, had to go after the session ended.

The war itself had taken a successful turn by 1704.[6] After two years of inconclusiveness and frustrations with the Dutch allies, Marlborough won the great victory of Blenheim in the summer of 1704 and Gibraltar had been captured by summer's end. The land warfare policy, if not vindicated, was at least popular and its critics could be dismissed from office with impunity.

In the third session which opened in the fall of 1704, the High Tories, without leadership in national office, came back prepared to tack their bill to the money bills to get it through Lords where it had been stopped twice before. They were mistaken in thinking that they had even the votes to ensure the tack, much less force Lords' assent. When the vote came on the tack, only 134 High Tories were willing to be tallied in the face of royal and governmental displeasure against almost double that many on the other side. The tack failed by such a wide margin because of the defection, or departure before the division, of erstwhile supporters of the bill—"Sneakers" as other High Tories called them. Undaunted by this defeat the "Tackers," as High Tories who voted for the tack were called thereafter, spent the

6. The best discussion of the war's significance in English politics during the period is Douglas Coombs, *The Conduct of the Dutch* (1958), pp. 49–51, and chaps. 3 and 4 in general.

rest of the parliamentary session obstructing business and attacking the queen's chief ministers. By March, 1705, even the queen was moved in her prorogation speech to reprove the "unreasonable humour and animosity, the fatal effects of which we have so narrowly escaped in this session."[7]

Just how serious the queen and government considered the threat of these "fatal effects" was demonstrated by the almost wholesale removal from public office of Tackers. Earlier dismissals of Rochester, Nottingham, and Seymour were moves toward eliminating Tory hotheads in office so that the government might get on with the war's prosecution without internal dissent. In 1704 Robert Harley had come in in the place of Nottingham as secretary of state for the southern department; Henry St. John, Harley's protégé, became secretary-at-war; and Thomas Mansell, another Harleyite, became comptroller in Seymour's place. At the end of the session certain Whigs, among them the Duke of Newcastle and Robert Walpole (but none of the Junto), were invited into the government to give it additional parliamentary support for pursuing what looked to be a victorious war.[8] When the last of these changes had been made, the queen on April 5, 1705, dissolved Parliament and shortly thereafter issued writs for the election of a new one.

After all that had happened—the cross-purposes of political ambitions and the confrontation of determined opinions over a basic issue—the general election could hardly have been a quiet one. It was made more turbulent by the propaganda cranked off the presses months before even the first contests took place. To quote Charles Leslie, "both town and country" were

7. Cobbett, VI, 437.

8. See Walcott, *English Politics*, pp. 111–114, on the ministerial changes in 1704–1705.

"filled . . . with multitudes of pamphlets and papers."[9] Leslie and his enemy, Defoe, contributed heavily to the volume with their new journals, the *Rehearsal* and *Review*, and with Tutchin's older *Observator* added a new force to partisan polemic. Now a writer could develop a distinct, consistent point of view over a period of weeks or even months and, hopefully, build or broaden support for it. In the pamphlet he could speak only once and the message might soon be lost in the babel accompanying an election. That journals did help create political bases is indicated by the desire of coffeehouse proprietors to stock papers for their patrons. In Northampton a woman who kept a coffeehouse frequented by Tories (coffeehouses were designated as Whig or Tory by the political persuasion of the clientele) covered her table with copies of *Dyer's Newsletter*, the *Rehearsal*, and other Tory pieces.[10] And in Norwich Defoe's *Review* was taken by the master of a local coffeehouse to satisfy his Whig patrons.[11]

Defoe had been at the ministry's service, or at least in one minister's service, for over a year by 1705.[12] Late in 1702 Harley,

9. *Rehearsal of Observator*, I, no. 44, May 26–June 2, 1705. Cited in later notes as *Rehearsal*. Bishop Burnet said: "Books were writ and dispersed over the nation with great industry" (*History of My Own Time*, V, 223). Another observer commented: "The lampoons fly as thick as hail in order to influence the approaching elections (British Museum Add. MSS 4743, f. 32v, cited in Cunnington, "The General Election of 1705," p. 24, n. 1). "Feuds were scarce ever higher, nor greater interest made," wrote one contemporary, "All the distinctions of parties were not confined to High and Low Church only, but tackers, sneekers and what not were continually trumped up" (Morgan, *English Political Parties*, p. 109).

10. *Observator*, IV, no. 11, May 5–9, 1705, and *Rehearsal*, I, no. 45, June 2–9, 1705.

11. Norgate, "Correspondence between Defoe and John Fransham," p. 261.

12. Three works might be consulted by anyone wishing to look further into the relationship between Harley and Defoe: Stevens, *Party Politics*, chap. 4; Paul Dottin, *Daniel Defoe et ses romans* (1924), Vol. I; and James Sutherland, *Daniel Defoe* (1950). Henry L. Snyder adds details to Harley's hiring of

already moving closer to Godolphin and away from Nottingham and Rochester, pressed Godolphin about the importance of the ministry's having a propagandist, "some discreet writer of the Government side," as he phrased it.[13] Godolphin in time agreed, acquiesced in Defoe's election, and left it up to Harley to oversee the matter.[14] It meant getting Defoe out of Newgate jail, and doing it inconspicuously since the Earl of Nottingham, also in the government, had put him there. This was in November, 1703. Allowing for a few weeks of preparation before the first publication of his *Review* on February 19, 1704, Defoe probably began work for Harley late in 1703 or early in 1704. It was the beginning of a relationship which lasted a decade, a relationship whose essential features are preserved in letters and memoranda but about which Defoe's contemporaries knew little. It was not a servile scribbler's role for Defoe. He often waited on Harley for money (always expecting more than he got), but he didn't need ideas or direction and turned out a prodigious quantity of copy for the occasional visits he made to Harley's backstairs. Defoe seemed to know what Harley wanted because he too believed in the Harleian scheme of moderation and consensus in government.[15] Harley, for his part, had money and needed Defoe's pen. It was a meeting of mutual needs.

Defoe's job as ministerial writer was to argue a new point of view, namely that the nation needed moderation, consensus, and stability at home and persistence against the French. The

---

Defoe (initially Harley wanted him as an agent in Scotland) in "Daniel Defoe, the Duchess of Marlborough, and the *Advice to the Electors of Great Britain*," pp. 53–62.

13. Stevens, p. 47.

14. Ibid.

15. Feiling, pp. 312–316, has a good sketch of Harley's political principles and goals. And there is an article by Angus McInnes, "The Political Ideas of Robert Harley," pp. 309–322, that is worth consulting.

policy was Harley's, the articulation of it Defoe's, and it had the support of Godolphin and Marlborough because it meant getting on with the war. As a policy it was more than an ad hoc propaganda theme for the general election of 1705. Defoe and Harley had been thinking about the threat to moderation and stability posed by the Occasional Conformity Bill long before the elections.[16] But the elections were a chance to broaden political support for the policy and strengthen the position of the ministry, and especially Harley, through the addition of M.P.'s sympathetic to the war and opposed to fierce factionalism.

Defoe hammered on the note that domestic strife would have fearful consequences:

> If we are Embroil'd here at Home, while we are at War Abroad; if by putting Gross and Illegal Affronts upon one another; if by the Constitution Jangling with it self we are Disabled from the War, the Confederacy broke, the Protestant Interest Abroad run down, the Dutch ruin'd, and the French Victorious. Pardon me, Gentlemen, I won't Answer for the People of England then when Universal Monarchy is obtain'd, and Europe submits to the Tyranny of the House of Bourbon, who are we to resist? What Proportion can this little Spot bear to the Triumphant Powers of Popery and French Government.[17]

---

16. See the letter of Defoe to Harley, November 2, 1704, H.M.C., Portland MSS, IV, 146–149. In the fall of 1704 Defoe was on a canvassing tour for Harley, "spreading principles of temper, moderation, and peace, through countries [counties] . . . and persuading all people that the Government is resolved to proceed by those rules" (Defoe to Harley, September 28, 1704, Portland MSS, IV, 137).

17. *Weekly Review of the Affairs of France,* II, no. 30, May 12, 1705. In the nineteenth issue on April 27 Defoe began the moderation theme; he continued it until June 16. Cited in later notes as the *Review*, as it was finally entitled in 1712.

He assailed the Tackers for creating that strife, charging that they "would venture losing the Money-Bill, Dissolving the House, Disabling the Queen, and breaking the Confederacy, rather than not pass the Occasional Bill."[18] They were, he said in the same issue, persecutors and men of blood. He scorned their claim that they were only attempting to secure the church.[19] If this was their intent, he said, they could have had the bill; but because they threatened persecution and imposed on the queen's promise to maintain the toleration, the Lords could not admit their bill. Now, pray, who is to be charged with exposing the church to danger? If the church was in danger, the Tackers neglected to protect it by insisting on such rigorous measures that the House could not accept the bill. "So that, in short, 'tis a Specious Outside to a State Intrigue, a Gilded Pill full of Poison, and Conceal'd Dangers."[20] Defoe meant that they were in league with papists, Jacobites, and nonjurors "to Destroy our Government, and Pull down the Church."[21] England, having so recently escaped from the danger in which the Tackers placed it, can scarcely wish to entrust these men again with its affairs. This would be putting "the Representing Knife" into the hands of madmen.[22] "Men of Peace, who promote this General Temper of Peace in the Nation, they are the Men we ought to Choose, to represent us in the Parliament; these are the Men that will keep us under God from all sorts of Foreign or Domestic Tyranny; that Wisely hold the Ballance between Contending Parties, and prevent the Eagerness of

18. Ibid., no. 25, May 1, 1705.
19. Ibid., no. 31, May 15, 1705.
20. Ibid.
21. Ibid., no. 33, May 19, 1705.
22. Ibid., no. 25, May 1, 1705.

Hot Men, on either side, running us on to Irrecoverable Confusions."[23]

Moderation, union, consensus—these were new ideas and strange ones for this reign. They were nonideological and nonpartisan, peculiar amidst hortative partisanship. And yet Defoe's was an electoral appeal. It was aimed at those whose hopes for the war's success were up after 1704 and who might be expected to be worried that the Tackers were jeopardizing its progress. Defoe, Harley, and the ministry were guessing that there were numbers of such people among both Whigs and Tories and that they might rally, for a while at least, to the government. For Harley this was risky business since he could not politically afford to estrange any Tories he might need in the future. So Defoe had to see him secretly and appear to be working only for the ministry.

Curiously, Defoe was not the only writer urging moderation and union. John Tutchin's *Observator* almost echoed Defoe's call for moderation: "Her Majesty's last speech from the throne [April 5, 1705] is a mark by which we may steer our course in our elections. The moderate man is the person we can depend on in our choice. Men of violent tempers and passions can never be masters of their own reason."[24] Do you choose well, he asked, when you choose members whose contentiousness thwarts the queen? Do you choose men who will maintain the constitution, our ancient laws and liberties, when you choose men who would disunite us and keep the Dissenters from serving the queen? What Tutchin wrote just before and during the elections was still good Whiggism. He denounced

23. Ibid., no. 24, April 28, 1705.

24. *Observator,* IV, no. 3, April 7–11, 1705; see also no. 8, April 25–28, 1705.

High Churchmen and their "arbitrary and slavish principles."[25] And he was not worried about extremism among Whigs, unlike Defoe. Indeed it was very clear that by moderate men he meant Whigs, but his moderation sounded very much like Defoe's, so much so that to their enemies they looked like allies.[26]

In a sense Defoe and the ministry back of him did have allies. The Junto lords and their friends in the parliamentary session of 1704–1705 had voted with the administration on all the important divisions for tactical rather than ideological reasons. The Junto had been without offices since 1702. When the Tory leaders went into opposition in 1703 and 1704 the Junto set out to make themselves indispensable allies of the ministry. They intended to make Godolphin pay them off with important governmental posts. They were doing this when they sided with the ministry on crucial votes in 1704–1705.[27] It was also part of the policy that Halifax asked Charles Davenant, erstwhile Tory pamphleteer, to write *Essays Upon Peace at Home and War Abroad* (1704), urging a truce among all parties to carry on the war.[28] Tutchin's moderation and union theme thus has antecedents and an explanation in Junto policy. This theme ties to-

---

25. Ibid.

26. *The Tackers Vindicated, or an Answer to the Whig New Black-List* (1705).

27. See Walcott, *English Politics*, pp. 114–115, on Junto policy.

28. See the article on Davenant in the *Dictionary of National Biography*, v, 549–550. Feiling, p. 371, n. 2, says that Godolphin saw and approved the work as well, providing a strong piece of evidence of a concert between ministry and Junto on the theme. In addition Halifax was in correspondence with Defoe in the spring and summer of 1705. He passed on money from a benefactor and hints for the *Review* to Defoe (Henry L. Snyder has shown that the donor was the Duchess of Marlborough in "Daniel Defoe and the *Advice to the Electors*," pp. 53–62). If only indirect ones, these are signs of Junto and ministerial cooperation.

gether a spate of other pamphlets written for the elections. The pamphlets were mainstream Whiggism of the previous decade but ended with a call for national unity. Typically, *Some Plain Observations Recommended to the Consideration of Every Honest Englishman* first dinned its readers with the Whig accusations of 1702—the Tories were Jacobites and pro-French because they had obstructed the business of William III's government and sabotaged the war effort—and then pressed for unity against the common enemy.[29] Like the *Observator*, it was obviously talking about unity on Whig terms, since it had already said Tory principles were subversive and pro-French, but it called for unity nonetheless.

Tutchin and the other (nameless) Whig writers had to accomplish two things to aid Junto policy. They had to muffle or dilute the straight Whiggism of 1702 so that it would key into the ministry's call for domestic peace and union. But the Junto lords also had to increase their forces in Commons to make Godolphin take them into the government. So the Whiggism in the propaganda had to be sufficiently discernible to help Whig, especially Junto Whig, candidates in the elections.[30] Doing both these things was not especially difficult. Several pamphlets and the *Observator* brought it off rather well. But as a concerted effort it did require some type of coordination or

---

29. See also *Tackers Toss'd in a Blanket; Character of a Tacker; A Serious Address to the Commoners of England; The Politicks of High Church: Or, a System of Their Principles About Government;* and *Seasonable Advice to the Electors*, all published in 1705.

30. As in *Plain French: or a Satyr upon the Tackers; Written to Caution and Direct English Freeholders in the Choice of a New Parliament; And Particularly the Electors in Buckinghamshire* (1705), which the Marquis of Wharton spent enough in publication costs to send through four editions, and enough copies undoubtedly to blanket the county. The pamphlet, incidentally, quotes Defoe's *Review* approvingly, again indicating some concert between Junto and ministerial propaganda campaigns.

management and reveals, if only dimly, the hand of the Junto in propaganda during the elections.

Tories sympathetic to the Tackers articulated the third point of view in the elections. They were a remnant of the triumphant coalition which had begun as allies and members of the new ministry shortly after the queen's accession, had still been leagued with the government during the general election of 1702, but had gone into opposition in the next two years over the Occasional Conformity Bill. Repeated defeats had not made them change their aims or shaken their belief in the importance of these aims. Indeed they only became more convinced that the crucial issue was the profaning of the church by "conformists," not the French threat. They were more determined to end occasional conformity. So singleminded had the adverse events of 1702–1705 and the attacks of Defoe and the Whig writers made them that all their propaganda centered on the tack as if they had all but forgotten the war against France. In part this mood and propaganda theme reflected the natural ideology of the Tackers' supporters, the bulk of whom were clergymen, mainly lower clergymen. As always when we begin to talk about a partisan view, the question is who instigated it. How much came from churchmen who wrote simply because they were genuinely worried about the church and wanted to awaken the nation to its peril? And how much came from writers retained by (or, like Sir Humphrey Mackworth, politically allied to) Nottingham, Rochester, and Seymour, who had staked everything on the Occasional Conformity Bill?[31]

Charles Leslie, the Tackers' ablest defender, was surely writ-

31. See the article on Mackworth in the *Dictionary of National Biography*, XII, 631–633. Dr. Drake's only known effort during these months was the *Memorial of the Church of England* (1705) which appeared too late—in mid-summer—to have had any influence on elections.

ing for the welfare of the church whose orders he had taken and for whose purity he had become a nonjuror after the revolution.[32] But was he, as Tutchin said, a hireling who got "a contribution from the High Church" for writing the *Rehearsal?*[33] Leslie denied that he got anything and said his only interest was in opening people's eyes. That may have been true. His livelihood for many years was a chaplaincy in the household of Edward Hyde, second Earl of Clarendon. But Clarendon was the elder brother of the Earl of Rochester, which opens up speculative possibilities. Clarendon, a nonjuror, had retired from politics after the revolution and had given up the political headship of the Hyde family to Rochester.[34] Undoubtedly Rochester knew Leslie. Leslie's superior talents and prolific writings denied him the anonymity or even the obscurity which some political writers had and which he probably wanted for himself. Could Rochester have commanded his services, or Nottingham through Rochester? Perhaps, although it was not necessary. Leslie, like Defoe, was a resourceful fellow who gave evidence later during his fugitive days of considerable initiative.[35] In any case what he wrote during the elections did not have to be coordinated with any complex political strategy. The strategy was simple—defend the Tackers. It had been forced on the High Tories because their opponents had so clearly thrown down the challenge to Tackers seeking reelection and because the war was going so well for the allies it could not be used as an issue. Significantly, though, Leslie and

---

32. See the article on Leslie in the *Dictionary of National Biography*, XI, 956–962.

33. Both Tutchin's charge and Leslie's reply are reported in the *Rehearsal*, I, no. 47, June 16–23, 1705.

34. Walcott, *English Politics*, p. 60.

35. See the *Dictionary of National Biography* for his activities on behalf of the Pretender.

Sir Humphrey Mackworth and other nameless men who wrote High Tory propaganda implemented the strategy with three common themes. The first was that the Tackers were not violent men but men of estates, the most respectable and responsible men of their counties. Their opponents were republicans, presbyterians, or "Sneakers,"[36] men of no principles. Since the success of the war hinged on the unity and strength of the church, the Tackers tried to pass the Occasional Conformity Bill to purge the church of its enemies and wipe out an offense to God which might cause England to lose the war.

Leslie contended that the Tackers had been singled out by the Whigs because they were the most important members of Parliament, most of them being knights of the shire, and because having gotten rid of them the Whigs could then deal easily with the rest of the nation. In the words of "Observator," the Whig spokesman in the *Rehearsal:*

> For this reason we use all endeavours to get them excluded in the ensuing elections. To which end we have legions of pamphlets, characters, Sing-songs, etc., ready to throw out day after day, among the Mobile, to keep them warm; wherein we assure them, that these Tackers are all of them Papishes and Jacobites, and have already sold their country to the French, tho' they have so great a stake in it! . . . But this is not all. We have emissaries . . . in all quarters through the kingdom, to back the circular letters we have sent everywhere; and to give the word at all elections, No Tacker, No Tacker! No High-Church-Man![37]

---

36. Those who at first supported the Occasional Conformity Bill but "sneaked" out before the division on the tack were attacked in *The Character of a Sneaker* (1705).

37. *Rehearsal*, I, no. 34, March 17–24, 1705. Also see *Tom Tell-Truths* (1705); *The Countryman's Remembrancer* (1705); *Rehearsal*, I, no. 35, March 24–31, 1705. Also the *Letter from a Member of Parliament to His Friend in*

Anti-Tackers, so the second theme went, were all republicans and presbyterians trying to recreate 1641 by first breaking down the established church from within. They opposed the Occasional Conformity Bill because it would keep them from gaining control of the church and the state although they masked their design under the cause of moderation. The failure of the bill stripped the church of its legal security and endangered the state as well. "Suppose," the *Rehearsal* said,

> an Enemy who had before sack'd and raz'd your city: and after peace [was] made, had made several attempts to betray and burn it: and shou'd desire leave now only to pull down your walls; alledging they were of no use to you, only hinder'd you from the free air; and besides, that it would be no invading of your property, for that he wou'd touch not one of your houses. No, upon his word he wou'd not. Only have it in his power![38]

This led into the third theme: that success in the war depended on internal unity and that the Tackers had tried to unify Englishmen under the church. "As Gentlemen saw a necessity of carrying on the War with Vigour on one side, so on the other they apprehended there was no way to secure the Establish'd Government, and to put an end to the Contention in the Kingdom, but by passing the Occasional Bill; and there

---

the Country (1705) written anonymously by Sir Humphrey Mackworth, deputy governor of the Mine Adventurers and a political friend of Sir Edward Seymour. Mackworth also wrote several other works during the period. He sat for Seymour's borough Totnes in the new Parliament.

38. *Rehearsal*, 1, no. 35, March 24–31, 1705. Also see *Presbyterian Loyalty* (1705); Henry Sacheverell's printed sermons, *Political Union* (1702) and *Rights of the Church of England Asserted* (1705); *The Case of Moderation and Occasional Communion* (1705); *A Dialogue or New Friendly Debate* (1705); *Letter From a Member of Parliament* (1704); *The Pretensions of the Church and its Enemies Stated* (1705).

was no way to pass that Bill, but by Consolidating the same with the Land Tax."[39] They also wanted to end an affront certain to bring God's disfavor upon England, another writer declared: "Do you think that meer raising of Men, Money and other necessary Provisions for War, will make our Armies Victorious, without God's Blessing?"[40] We dare not risk the wrath of God; the occasional conformists must be reformed or excluded, lest they bring a curse upon us.

What configurations had occurred in political ideologies and what changes in propaganda techniques or devices had taken place since 1702? There were no new issues in 1705. The furor over the tack was a species of the old contention about the safety of the church, although the tack was unique in its own way because it gave concreteness and immediacy to the older abstraction. Rather than two ideological patterns there were three. Each possessed a fairly high degree of coherence which suggests planning. Two of the views were tactically allied: the Junto Whig and the ministerial. The latter was really the most significant of the three from the perspective of the student of propaganda because it introduced an element of pragmatism into partisan propaganda. Ideological concerns were never all-consuming in the party writings tied together by the theme of moderation; indeed the theme was to show the madness to which hard-line partisan ideology could lead. Both the theme and the devices which implemented it were new to the reign of Anne and persisted until the end of the reign. Traditional Whig propaganda devices were subordinated to a considerable degree to the implementation of the theme of moderation. In techniques there was greater carry-over in the High Tory or

39. *A Letter From a Member of Parliament.* See also *A Dialogue or New Friendly Debate*, and *The Reviewer Reviewed* (1705).

40. *A Dialogue or New Friendly Debate.*

High Church view. The necessity of defending the tack required adapting these techniques to the circumstances but not radical revision, except that writers stopped condemning the Continental land policy and tacitly accepted it by saying that the Occasional Conformity Bill would produce a national front and shorten the war.

Party writers and party leaders at Westminster thought the tack was a crucial issue. But did voters think so? Many people knew, even before the vote on the tack, what they were going to do when election time came. The High Tories of Derbyshire were vowing as early as January, 1704, never to vote again for Thomas Coke because he was against the Occasional Conformity Bill.[41] And others feared the outcome of elections, so strong had feelings become since the rather placid general election of 1702: "I cannot but tremble at the thought of a Tory H of Co[mmons] . . . I shall not think it very comfortable living in Dorsets when the T[ories] have got the possession of the country, & can let loose the C[our]t or Ch[urch] on those they please at pleasure."[42]

For the first time in the period of Anne's reign propaganda was aimed at specific contests, at the Middlesex, Buckingham, Oxford, and Suffolk county contests and London, Exeter, and Durham, just to mention some. Durham's, so the Whig member thought, was significantly affected by propaganda.[43] He was certain that the hostility of *Dyer's Newsletter* had cost him clerical votes, especially those of the cathedral clergy which had gone to his fellow member, a Tacker. He won reelection

41. H.M.C., Cowper MSS, III, 20, 29–30.

42. Holmes, *British Politics*, p. 409.

43. Cunnington, "General Election of 1705," p. 187. See passim for the other elections mentioned above in which propaganda was connected with specific contests.

nevertheless, but narrowly. Suffolk's was close too and hard-fought; each side made extravagant charges against the other and mustered every available voter. One of the Tacker candidates was a Jacobite, said the *London Post*, and had the help of Charles Leslie and county Catholics.[44] The *Rehearsal*, consistent with its policy, thumped away at the theme that the Tackers were gentlemen and had the support of the leading gentlemen of Suffolk. On the other side was "a scoundrel medley," a "rabble of Presbyterians, Independents, Anabaptists, Quakers, Papists, and Moderation brothers." They polled the "Lame, blind, and all that could only speak," while the Tackers' party were respectable and orderly and augmented by a body of over two hundred clergy.[45]

What happened in contests in the freer constituencies—the universities, counties and larger boroughs—those most open to issues and appeals to the public side of party? What impact did issues have—particularly the tack since it symbolized partisan ideological differences—and is there a pattern to the results that could be assigned to the impact of ideology? Tackers did lose more heavily there than they did among the safer seats, which seems to reiterate the experience of 1702 that electoral trends were likely to run stronger in open constituencies.[46] The difference between the rate of losses in the open and closed constituencies is not as radically different as it appeared to be in

44. *London Post*, no. 29, May 4, 1705.

45. *Rehearsal*, I, no. 42, May 12–19, 1705.

46. The actual figures for the two types of constituencies were these: in the 1702 Parliament seventy-five Tackers had represented closed constituencies and fifty-nine the freer constituencies. After the 1705 elections fifty-one sat for closed and thirty-nine for freer constituencies. The numerical losses were twenty from the freer and twenty-four from closed seats. The biographical work Miss Cunnington did for the "General Election of 1705" was invaluable in making these computations. As in the last chapter, I used constituencies suggested by Robert Walcott and discussed in the introduction above.

1702, but it is enough to maintain the distinction between the two and to admit the possibility that the difference resulted from issues.

Thirty-four percent of the Tackers who had to face the larger electorates did not get their old seats back. In many of these elections, we know or can safely assume that propaganda had been disseminated. Middlesex voters, for instance, had surely seen most of the partisan literature published in London. Both the *Observator* and *Dyer's Newsletter* took a special interest in the county elections, and the mob at polling time at least gave evidence of knowing what the ideological issues were. Both sitting members were Tackers; one had represented the county since 1698.[47] But the county had a large contingent of Dissenters, many of whom were enfranchised.[48] On polling day a mob gathered to jeer the Tory candidates with epithets of Jacobite, nonjuror, Perkinite—all accusations of loyalty to France and the exiled Stuarts rather than England and the reigning line. *Dyer's Newsletter* was piqued at hearing that a considerable bloc of Dissenters turned out to vote against the Tackers, "as they have done," it noted sourly, "against the Church's interest all England over."[49] After the two Tackers had been turned out by the poll (both having lost by about three hundred votes out of a total of some twenty-four hundred votes cast), the new members were escorted the ten miles into London where the procession wound through the streets and plied the river to shouts of "No Jacobites," "No French Government," "No Wooden Shoes."[50]

---

47. Walcott, *English Politics*, p. 56.

48. See Cunnington, pp. 195–203, for an analysis of the Dissenters' strength and its relationship to the outcome of the elections.

49. H.M.C., Portland MSS, IV, 188, 190, quoting the issues for May 17 and May 31, 1705.

50. Trevelyan, *England under Queen Anne* (1932), II, 27–28.

Including the results from other elections Tackers lost twenty of the relatively open seats, but they kept thirty-nine of that type. One reason seems to be that they held their own in a number of traditional Tory strongholds among the freer constituencies when there were determined efforts to whip up pro-Tacker sentiments and get out pro-Tacker voters. Issues and propaganda figured prominently in most of the Oxfordshire elections. The significant contests were the county, university, and city ones because of the larger electorates, the circulation of propaganda, and the interest of major politicians in the candidates.[51] In Oxford City, Rochester, Nottingham, and Weymouth backed Tackers against a couple of Whigs, one of whom had the support of the Duchess of Marlborough. At the university, a High Church bastion, Rochester dropped a friend, Clarke, to support Bromley and Whitlock because they were Tackers and Clarke was not.[52] Tackers stood for the shire as well and the three other borough seats in the county.

The struggle began well before the elections while the old Parliament was still sitting. Late in March the High Tory *Rehearsal* professed horror at "hearing" that Whigs and Low Churchmen were threatening to shoot all the Tacker candidates. It printed a circular letter they supposedly sent through the county: *The Names of the Tackers for Oxfordshire, who are Pensioners of France, and Ought to be Shot Through the Head if They Pretend to Appear at the Ensuing Election.*[53] Tackers, the paper went on to say, were not extremists after all. They were respectable, responsible men. The violence was all coming from subversives who wanted to eliminate the

---

51. See Cunnington, pp. 126–127, for the documentation on the Oxford elections.

52. Holmes, *British Politics*, p. 277n.

53. *Rehearsal*, I, no. 35, March 24–31, 1705.

church and the monarchy. At the same time someone in London with Whiggish notions and a desire for some Whig victories in Oxford printed a broadsheet satirizing the "Oxfordshire Nine" in catchy if unmemorable verse.[54] The results, after the actual polling, must have been heartening to High Tories since things were not going nearly so well elsewhere. Tackers won the county seats, the university, and carried the city by whopping majorities, more than two to one against the Whigs. They picked up an additional seat in the other borough elections.

Admittedly the importance of propaganda in the outcome of the contests is highly arguable. The city, county, and university electorates were no doubt literate—surely the latter was—and many of them were exactly the voters for whom Leslie intended the *Rehearsal*. If the clergy canvassed for the Tackers there as they did elsewhere the journal would have had a goodly number of hearers besides its normal readers in the county.[55] By some figures clergymen in other counties were polling for Tackers at a rate of nearly five out of seven.[56] And many of them did not think it unscrupulous to catechize politically while they were instructing religiously.[57] At the same time

54. The Duchess of Marlborough might have had a hand in it. In 1708 she helped compose a pamphlet: Henry L. Snyder, "Daniel Defoe and *Advice to the Electors*," pp. 53–62.

55. In the first chapter I cited the Scarborough priest who in 1710 took the *Examiner* around on parish visits: H.M.C., Portland MSS, IV, 641, J. Durden to Robert Harley, December 5, 1710.

56. It was said that in Berkshire 119 out of 140 clergymen polled against the Whig candidate who won easily anyway, and in Kent, Defoe reported, 150 out of 318 clerics voted for the Tackers (see the *Observator*, IV, no. 16, May 23–26, 1705, and the *Review*, II, no. 37, May 29, 1705, and no. 44, June 14, 1705).

57. One parson, according to the *Observator*, IV, no. 9, April 28–May 2, 1705, said "the Devil take me if it be not a greater sin to poll against the Tackers than to murder my own father." The parish priest in Abingdon, said

Oxfordshire had long been a Tory refuge, and while political literature may have changed some minds on one side or the other, it surely reflected existing prejudices more than it reversed attitudes. Perhaps its function, not only for the Tory interest but the Whig as well, was to reflect and strengthen partisan affinities. The Oxford Tackers needed a strong showing. They were preponderant in the county and had said all along that they were gentlemen of the best estates. Their appeal was social, class-oriented to the landed of Oxfordshire, to unite them behind the Tackers. The Whigs really had not a chance at most of the counties' seats, but they were emboldened to try because the court had repudiated the High Tories and was taking special notice of the Oxfordshire elections. These strategies at any rate square with the extant pieces of propaganda both of which were stiff tonics for the faithful and more than mere passive resonance of existing political opinions. They were tendentious to stronger feelings, commitments, and electoral efforts by both groups of partisans. In this instance the High Tory forces mustered enough strength to dominate the county and help offset losses elsewhere in the country.

Normally the Tackers could have counted on losing few contests for what were generally safer seats, the smaller boroughs with narrow franchises. But the rate of losses there was 32 percent, a rather substantial lot of failures. Twenty-four of the seventy-five who had sat in the old Parliament were not in the new one. Why were there so many losses in generally undisturbed seats? Did issues penetrate even these electoral fastnesses? The tack certainly was the sort of issue which could break into the localism of normally closed elections. Abingdon,

---

the *Observator*, pretended to have the power to forgive sins and exercised this power only in behalf of those sharing his political sentiments (ibid., and no. 11, May 5–9, 1705).

for example, was not usually troubled at election time. Its incumbent, Sir Simon Harcourt, solicitor general, should have won reelection handily, except that in Commons he apparently had not taken a strong enough stand early enough against the tack. He had opposition which was strongly anti-Tacker and which had the support of the *Observator*. Henry St. John tried to do what he could for Harcourt but was not much help, as he wrote Harley, because there was "so much merit in being against the Tack, whatever some wise men may think, that Neville was not to be opposed."[58] But Abingdon, although not a unique case, was not really typical either, because ideology alone did not often make the difference in contests in the narrower, smaller constituencies. As in every general election, the greater and lesser political managers within government and without bullied and pleaded and commanded and spent to make themselves powerful in the new House of Commons. And their activities undoubtedly go farther toward explaining the high rate of Tacker losses in the controlled seats than national issues alone.

The queen's chief ministers marshaled the full electoral powers of the crown well before the elections by making changes among local royal officials to install men of whose loyalties they were sure.[59] All the principal Tories who had leaned toward the Tackers—Buckingham, Granville, Dysart, Winchelsea, and Guildford—were turned out of their lord lieutenancies. And Sir Peter Shakerley, another Tacker, was replaced as governor of Chester Castle. Such changes made a difference: Lord Westmorland, newly appointed governor of Dover Castle and deputy governor of the Cinque Ports, took his electoral duties seriously, going "through all the Cinque

58. H.M.C., Portland MSS, IV, 180, St. John to Harley, May 15, 1705.

59. See Cunnington, pp. 60–76, for a full discussion of these changes.

Ports to prepare for an election which was soon after to be, and with such success that the members were allmost all changed to the Prin^ls I was of."[60] He made certain that the only Tacker among the members from the Cinque Ports was not reelected. Government leaders further sought to enhance their position by employing their own personal interests in elections. Godolphin's connections in the West Country helped in the election of at least twenty-nine supporters to the Parliament of 1705.[61] When his were added to the efforts of the Marlboroughs and Robert Harley,[62] the queen's chief ministers went back to Westminster with some twenty-eight more supporters than they had had in the Commons of 1702.

Whig leaders successfully recouped losses which their electoral interests had suffered in the general election of 1702. The Marquis of Wharton alone spent over £12,000 on the elections of 1705, intervening successfully on behalf of over thirty candidates.[63] His primary interest was in the elections in Buckinghamshire, where his chief estates lay.[64] His fortunes in any election year can be gauged by the success he enjoyed in that county. In 1702 he could count only six supporters from the county; in 1705 this number increased to ten. In 1702 only one of Wharton's nominees for the county seats had won: Robert Dormer, a locally important squire, had been defeated by a

60. Ibid., p. 66.

61. See Walcott, *English Politics*, pp. 53, 218–219, for a discussion of Godolphin's electoral interest. For the opposition he faced from Sir Edward Seymour's interest see Cunnington, pp. 80–101; Norman Sykes, "The Cathedral Chapter of Exeter and the Election of 1705," pp. 260–272.

62. See Cunnington, pp. 122–132, and Walcott, *English Politics*, p. 115.

63. Sir Richard Steele, *Memoirs of Thomas, Marquis of Wharton*, p. 41 (quoted in Cunnington, p. 152).

64. For Wharton and the Buckinghamshire elections see Cunnington, pp. 160–163. As a basis for comparison, also see Walcott's analysis of the 1702 election in *English Politics*, pp. 229–232. For Wharton's efforts in other elections see Cunnington, pp. 164–165.

Tory. Dormer, however, stood again in 1705 and won. And so did Sir Richard Temple, Wharton's electoral ally in the county, who had himself failed of reelection in 1702.[65] Wharton's Junto allies did as well in the elections, so that in the new Parliament the Junto Whigs mustered sixty-four members, an increase of twenty over the number in the old House of Commons.[66] The fortunes of the Duke of Somerset, another Whig leader, are also instructive. Engaged in a rivalry in Wiltshire with a local Tory family, Somerset also got opposition from the church in this election. But he still won two seats at Marlborough, seats he could not get for nominees in 1702. So he, as well as the other Whig leaders, had much more local influence than he had had three years before.[67]

High Tory or pro-Tacker leaders were not idle during this election, but they had lost, publicly lost, the favor of the queen and seemingly alienated a powerful segment of the country by their policies. Some of them, nonetheless, managed to do rather well. Sir Edward Seymour, despite the inroads of Godolphin in the West Country, still took back with him to Westminster a number of men who looked to him for leadership. The extent of the Tory losses is revealed by a comparison of the sizes of certain connections before and after the election of 1705. The supporters of the Earl of Rochester and Sir Edward Seymour

65. In note 30 above is cited the pamphlet *Plain French*, which was directed at the county elections and named Dormer and Temple. It went through at least four editions, but I could not find a reference to it in accounts of the county contests. It must have been the work of Wharton or friends and would seem to have been an attempt to supplement the personal electoral appeal Wharton was so famous for making.

66. Walcott, *English Politics*, p. 115.

67. For the Wiltshire election see Great Britain, Historical Manuscripts Commission, Report on the MSS of the Marquis of Ailesbury, pp. 189ff. Cited in later notes as H.M.C., Ailesbury MSS. For the efforts of other Whig peers see Cunnington, pp. 166–173.

were the most drastically thinned out: in the Parliament of 1702 they had numbered sixty-six; after the elections this number shrank to forty. The Earl of Nottingham had had fifty supporters in the old Parliament, but in the new one he had only thirty-nine. And the other Tories, those not associated with either of these two groups, had totaled at least 152 in 1702 but dropped in number to 126.[68] Another way of analyzing High Tory losses is to recall the fate of the Tackers. One hundred thirty-four voted for the tack; slightly more than 30 percent of them were not reelected.

Comparing the returns from the two kinds of constituencies and the fortunes of the Tackers there, which area of electoral activity made the most difference in the outcome? Obviously the largest bloc of reelected Tackers came from the smaller, narrower seats; so did most of the supporters of the ministry and the Whigs. But all three elements had compelling strategic reasons for electoral campaigns aimed at both kinds of seats. With the government and Whigs making inroads into controlled seats held by Tackers, it became more important to the High Tories to win as many of the more open seats as possible. The ministry, not knowing how well it would do in the closed constituencies, also needed as many of the open seats as it could pick up to hold the deciding bloc in Commons. The Junto Whigs could expect to do better in the smaller constituencies since their prospects for greater influence in government were strong. They could not afford to lose decisive votes in Commons by ignoring contests for the open seats because they were bidding for a greater share of ministerial posts. The margin of returns for pursuing the more ideologically oriented votes in

68. See Walcott, *English Politics*, p. 115, for a tabular comparison of the elections of 1702 and 1705.

the open constituencies was indeed small, but it could be a decisive margin, as political leaders from the three major blocs seem to have figured.

In any event the tone of the new House of Commons was perceptibly changed. The moderate ministerial Tories and the Whigs possessed a majority large enough to insure the success of the policies of Godolphin, Marlborough, and Harley. These ministers could now push on with the war and deal with the coming crisis in the relation of England to Scotland, confident that a working relationship between ministerial Tories and the Whigs would free them from the serious effects of High Tory harassment. But in this relationship there lay the seeds of future discord. After their contribution to the defeat of the Tackers, the Whigs became increasingly impatient to receive their share of policy-making posts. This factor, and the attempt of Godolphin and Marlborough to retain in their own hands the control of national affairs while maintaining ties with the Whigs by necessary concessions, set the pattern of party history for the next few years.

The General Election of 1708

III The most important question in English politics between the general elections of 1705 and 1708 was whether the Godolphin ministry would have to take the Whigs in to be able to carry on the government's program in Commons. By the election of 1708 the government seemed to have little choice but to bring important Whigs into the cabinet; the election results made it necessary. But the general election itself was singularly uneventful—there was less propaganda and less public interest than in any other election of the reign. One explanation is that the records have not survived. This is not really satisfactory, however, since the other elections are relatively well documented. The most satisfactory explanation is to be found in the party politics of 1705–1708 which explain both the character of the general election and the fluidity of partisan lines in the election propaganda.

After the general election of 1705 the movement of the ministry toward the Whigs, particularly the Junto Whigs, became so pronounced as to give Robert Harley and his moderate Tory friends serious misgivings. Harley protested with increasing frequency and warmth the trend events seemed to be taking.[1] But Godolphin disagreed with Harley's contention that the

1. Harley wrote Godolphin: "I dread the thoughts of running from the extreme of one faction to another, which . . . renders the Government like a door which turns both ways to let in each party as it grows triumphant, and in truth this is the real parent and nurse of our factions here" (Great Britain, Historical Manuscripts Commission, Report on the MSS of the Marquis of Bath at Longleat, Wiltshire, I, 181, Harley to Godolphin, September 10, 1707. Cited in later notes as H.M.C., Bath MSS).

moderates, both Tory and Whig, were the only reliable support for his administration. The queen herself became so alarmed at the prospect of a Whig-dominated administration that in late 1707 or early 1708 she sent secretly to Harley, indicating that she wished him to organize a government of moderates.[2] Harley tried to do what she wished, but his plans to assemble a new ministry without Godolphin and Marlborough fell through when the Cabinet Council to a man refused to serve without the duke. Harley resigned his secretaryship.[3] His one last hope, that the Tories would make such gains in the coming general election that Godolphin and Marlborough could not turn to the Whigs, vanished with the attempted Jacobite raid on Scotland in the spring.[4] Harley's difficult problem of repairing the deep-seated divisions between the High and moderate Tories became for the time insoluble with the psychological shock the Tories suffered at the Pretender's invasion.

The problems of the government did not vanish with Harley's resignation, however, because the Junto Whigs, convinced that a show of force was necessary to get all the offices they wanted, had committed themselves several months before to a policy of limited opposition to the government. At the beginning of the 1707–1708 session of Parliament they had joined the High Tories in attacking the admiralty and its head, who was

---

2. In January or February of 1708 Anne was telling Archbishop Sharp of York that "she meant to change her measures, and give no countenance to the Whig Lords but that all the Tories, if they would, should come in, and all Whigs likewise that would show themselves to be in her interests, should have favour" (Thomas Sharp, *The Life of John Sharp, Archbishop of York*, 1825, I, 323).

3. See Godfrey Davis, "The Fall of Harley in 1708," pp. 246–254, and Walcott, *English Politics*, pp. 143–146.

4. See Winston Churchill, *Marlborough: His Life and Times*, III (1936), chap. 18, for the Pretender's abortive raid.

Marlborough's brother.[5] They had charged the admiralty with graft and neglect in the loss of merchant shipping to French privateers, and they had kept an inquiry into the charges going throughout the session. They had also allowed the High Tories to maul the ministry badly in an investigation into the defeat of the British expeditionary force in Spain at Almanza, intervening only at the last minute on the government's side. Godolphin had every reason to worry that the Junto would intensify their pressure on the government during the elections. He knew they probably could get away with it because the Tories were too weak to capitalize on the temporary disunity in the governmental-Whig alliance.

All these circumstances shaped the propaganda of 1708. It was particularly important that Harley did not take Defoe with him when he went into opposition. Why he did not neither he nor Defoe ever divulged. If he foresaw his eventual return, he may have thought Defoe ultimately more credible to the commercial and trading interests if he did not take him into opposition. Or he could have been so nonplussed by the invasion attempt's following so close on his defeat that he could not think through an ideological strategy. Whatever the reason, Harley had no one to write for him, since the *Rehearsal*'s High Toryism was not his brand of ideology. Defoe remained with a ministry whose leaders did not fully appreciate his talents. Godolphin had never thought the press worth the attention Harley gave it, and he did not have the time for its assiduous cultivation.

Not unnaturally, therefore, the strongest piece of progovernmental propaganda on the issue of the Pretender's abortive invasion of Scotland, one of the primary propaganda issues of the

5. See Walcott, *English Politics*, pp. 132–143.

election, was not even commissioned by the ministry. It was Sarah Churchill, Duchess of Marlborough, who thought the government was not answering its critics on the invasion very well, who first conceived of the *Advice to the Electors, Occasioned by the Intended Invasion from France* and wrote it with the aid of her political advisor, Arthur Maynwaring.[6] The strength of the *Advice* was that it linked the only popular issue of the election to one for which banalities and conventional rhetoric often sufficed, even though Tories were neurotic at its mention—Jacobitism.

It was obvious, argued the *Advice*, that the Pretender would not have come without intelligence and promises of aid, and "if it be certain that some of the Tory-Party were actually engag'd in inviting the Pretender; and if it is not so much as suspected, that one Man of the Whigs was in the Design of the Invasion, this Consideration alone should be sufficient to determine the Choice of all the honest Free-holders in Great Britain." Whigs, the writers continued, had no reason to aid the Pretender. They had by precept and deed committed themselves to the revolution settlement and the Protestant succession. But Tories who "oppos'd the late King's [William's] coming to the Throne, and could not bring their Consciences, without great Difficulty, to own his Government" and who joined with papists to return Tackers to the last Parliament, among other things, did have a suspicious past. It could only have been they who invited or lured the Pretender over. So said the duchess and Maynwaring concisely and bitingly.

Defoe for the ministry dwelt on the same theme in the *Review*. Perhaps for that reason he caused less consternation and

6. See Snyder, "Daniel Defoe and the *Advice to the Electors*," pp. 53–62.

commotion than did the authors of the *Advice*.[7] Defoe actually got his views in print about a week before the *Advice* was published. So similar were his arguments and theirs that one suspects prior consultation or borrowing, but there is nothing to validate that suspicion. The duchess and Maynwaring were noted for their Whiggism but not for their support of the ministry at that time, but Defoe was openly a ministerial propagandist. He charged that the Tories' cries of mismanagement, of the falling off of trade, of exhausted funds, the deterioration of the navy and heavy losses at sea had created division at home and given the French reason to think that an invasion by the Pretender would succeed.[8]

As usual, Tories either ignored or made only feeble, ineffectual replies to the charge that they were Jacobites,[9] but, unlike their experience in other elections, they did not have to answer the charge by themselves. The *Observator*, reflecting the Junto's campaign to harass the ministry until it gave them additional seats in the Cabinet Council, took at least two issues during the elections to distinguish between patriotic and disloyal Tories.[10] It argued that there was an important difference between Tories who had accepted the revolution settlement and Jacobites (and papists) who obviously had not. And it took the position that crying Jacobitism was a ploy by the *Review* and the *Advice to the Electors* to turn popular attention away from the lack of defense preparations against the Pretender and the

7. See the *Review*, v, no. 6, April 10, 1708; no. 8, April 15, 1708; no. 11, April 22, 1708; no. 13, April 27, 1708.

8. Ibid., no. 14, April 29, 1708.

9. See, for example, *Honest Advice to the Electors of Great Britain in the Present Choice of Their Representatives* (1708), which protested Tory loyalty on the invasion issue.

10. *Observator*, VII, nos. 24, 25, May 5–8, 8–12, 1708.

government's mismanagement of Scottish affairs generally. It is true that no Junto spokesman had said these specific things in the last Parliament, but the limited harassment of the ministry was Junto policy.

We have speculated in earlier chapters about an apparent Junto influence on the *Observator*. In past elections it had tended to replicate Junto parliamentary arguments. It did so to a high degree during the 1708 election, even though the editorship of the paper had changed since 1705. John Tutchin had died in prison in September, 1707 (as the result of a beating by thugs hired by someone in the government, it was said), and the paper had passed into obscure hands, although they were still Whiggish and pro-Junto hands it would seem.[11] In any case those tenuous relations between the *Observator*'s managers and the Junto lords become much clearer when one examines a second issue of the elections, the alleged maladministration of the Godolphin ministry. The Junto had hammered especially hard at the admiralty; so did the *Observator*, although it did broaden to a wider critique of administrative policies. Mismanagement of the navy, so it said, permitted the French to inflict ruinous losses on English merchant shipping, threaten the nation, and escape as easily as they did after the invasion attempt. "I hope our Merchants, who have had such ruinous Losses, and our other Traders, who are sensible how much our Commerce is sunk, will now take Care to Chuse such Men as may make a thorough Enquiry into all the Causes of those Things."[12] Least likely to do that, it went on, were placemen or government supporters, who had prevented such an inquiry in the last Parliament because they thought more of loyalty to

11. See Stevens, *Party Politics*, p. 10.

12. *Observator*, VII, no. 22, April 28–May 1, 1708. See also no. 16, April 7–10, 1708; no. 21, April 24–28, 1708; no. 30, May 26–29, 1708.

the government than the interests of the whole nation and who therefore stood in the way of a free Parliament. Commercial interests and a free Parliament went together—a "free" one, the paper implied, having as few ministerial supporters as possible.[13] This was refurbished, classic Whiggism; freedom of elections, an independent Parliament, and the primacy of commercial interests were scarcely new ideas to men whose fathers and grandfathers had first heard them. But the *Observator* was building up to more than ideological exhortation by connecting maladministration, commercial decline, and packed Parliaments. People were already beginning to talk in the same breath about "disappointments abroad" and the sorry state of trade.[14] The journal wanted to bend this stream of thinking onto the ministry, but only for the period of the elections. The position of the paper was still that the war needed to be decisively won and so the stirring up of antiwar feelings or any implacable antiministerial opposition had to be avoided. What the journal wanted to do instead was cause sufficient disaffection among commercially employed voters to show the ministry that the Junto was indispensable. Surgical precision of that kind is always difficult to achieve in the manipulation of public opinion. Indeed it may be impossible. About how well the *Observator* succeeded we shall speculate later.

Defoe tried to rebut the *Observator* by cutting through to what undoubtedly was the heart of the matter: the Junto's desire for power. "What can all this Clamour mean," he asked, "and what is the Effect of it; but to lay all the blame of Mis-

13. Ibid., no. 21, April 24–28, 1708, and nos. 26, 27, 28, May 12–22, 1708.

14. One contemporary wrote: "Wee are much concern'd here for our disappointments abroad & for deadness of trade & Want of Money at home, wee shall go belly deep I am afraid if wee do not ly fast next session" (Coombs, *The Conduct of the Dutch*, p. 168).

carriages upon the Party now entrusted, in order to make the Nation uneasie with them, that a new Set of Men may come in their Places?"[15] The ministry, he confessed, had made honest mistakes; there had probably been deficiencies and ill conduct in the administration of the navy and he hoped that the persons responsible would be punished. But should this be a reason to turn a ministry out of office, he asked? "No, No, Gentlemen, be ye Tories or High Flyers, or be Whigs or Low Church, or what you will . . . you act against not your Duty only, but your Interest . . . for in the Design of deposing this Ministry lies hid the Ambuscade of Jacobitism, Tyranny, Bondage and Destruction."[16] Scare words were not infrequently Defoe's introduction to his moderation or consensus theme first expressed on Harley's behalf in 1705. It consisted of the argument that the country could not afford political factionalism and that only a coalition of moderates such as the Godolphin ministry could prevent the disintegration of domestic stability. The choice in the elections lay between men who would strengthen this coalition and maintain order and those who would pursue partisan interests. "If you choose Men that have a Sense of Liberty, a Sense of the Advantage of the Laws, and of a Government that adheres to them, and governs by them, you will be secure and they too. . . . If you choose Mercenaries [Defoe obviously was referring to the Junto Whigs] . . . they will be drawn in to joyn with a Party that will destroy you."[17]

Underlying the importance of the issue of maladministration in the elections was the question of the war. This question loomed large over the political situation all through Queen

15. *Review*, IV, no. 164, February 28, 1708.

16. Ibid., no. 164, February 28, 1708; no. 167, March 6, 1708; V, nos. 24, 25, May 22, 25, 1708.

17. Ibid., V, no. 30, June 5, 1708.

Anne's reign. After the auspicious victories of Blenheim in 1704 and Ramillies in 1706, the year 1707 was one of almost unmitigated disaster for the allies, and, if we may believe one scholar, "with its many setbacks and disappointments enthusiasm for the war amongst the majority of politically active Englishmen disappeared irrevocably."[18] Now there was only the desire to finish the war and end the drain of men and money. And there was rising bitterness over how little the allies seemed to be doing. Although these attitudes were not fully developed by the election of 1708, they were strong enough to enable the Tories to begin to hint openly, as they did in the last session of the Parliament of 1705, that the government had an interest in keeping the war going and that it could have had a peace treaty in 1705 if it had wanted one.

Defoe's job as ministerial apologist was to allay this growing war-weariness and to assuage English antagonism toward the allies. It was a difficult task and a new one for electoral purposes. In 1705 the prospects for victory had seemed auspicious and arguing for the war had not really been necessary. Defoe would continue to say what he had said in 1708 until Harley replaced Godolphin and it began to look as if it were safe to make peace with France. Any hastily executed peace would only bring later wars; the French had to be decisively defeated and dislodged from the Spanish throne, and the surest way to win was to fight in the Low Countries. The ministry had argued this strategy in 1702 and pursued it subsequently; Defoe adopted it substantially.[19] Irony seemed to be one of his favorite techniques in handling the war's inconclusiveness: "What," he asked, "signifies Truth or Liberty, if we have but Peace....

18. Coombs, p. 58.

19. *Advice to the Electors* also argued this strategy, as befitted a work written by the wife of the Duke of Marlborough.

What if you had no Trade, you should have Peace; what if you had no Manufactures, yet you should have Peace; what signifies it to us, who has Spain, or who has America." If you want peace—"French Peace, Popish Peace, Any Peace, if it be but PEACE"—Defoe concluded, elect Tories and High Flyers and you will have it.[20] The charge he had made in 1705 against the Tackers he repeated in defending the allies: the agitation and complaints against the allies were really aimed at dividing and weakening the nation, and he implied that such action was treasonable.

On the question of the war, the *Observator* swerved from its antiministerial tone back to a position supporting the ministry, that the conclusion to the war must not come until the Spanish monarchy was held by the Austrian line and the French had renounced the Stuart Pretender's claim to Britain. Otherwise there would only be future wars. So it advised the reader to "Chuse Men of true Revolution-Principles" who would be for carrying "on the War with such Vigor, as may conclude in an honourable Peace; by which the Hannover Succession may be effectually secur'd; the Ballance of Europe restor'd."[21] Like Defoe, the authors of the *Observator* had not argued this position before, but the war had come to require justifying and the writers and backers of the Whig paper held to a hard line against the French until the war was ended by Tory hands five years later.

Not much was written by Tories on any of the issues during the election, as the preceding paragraphs have shown. And they had very little to say about the war, compared to the ministerial

---

20. *Review*, v, no. 22, May 18, 1708. See also on this issue, iv, no. 166, March 4, 1708.

21. *Observator*, vii, no. 31, May 29–June 2, 1708; no. 21, April 24–28, 1708.

and Junto-Whig presses. *Honest Advice to the Electors of Great Britain* wondered whether the inconclusiveness of the Continental land policy had been offset by overseas trade and commercial expansion (pure irony in the light of the war's disruption of trade) and hinted that the ministry and the Whigs wanted to keep the war going: "When the next Parliament meets . . . it may be it will not be amiss, to examine, whether there might not have been a reasonable peace had, after the glorious victory at Ramilly; and whether it were by Whig or Tory Council, that it was not hearken'd to." The *Rehearsal* was more explicit; it denounced war profiteers and declared that there could be no peace until "Men grow Just and Prefer the Public Good to their own Private Interests."[22] In the *Rehearsal* Charles Leslie probably was just cutting at the ministry and the Whigs; the war was apparently not very significant to him. But *Honest Advice* was putting forward a point of view which had been heard before. The Earl of Nottingham, and possibly the Earl of Rochester, had in the election propaganda of 1702 bitterly assailed the Continental land policy of the Duke of Marlborough. They favored a naval overseas campaign to seize France's colonies if a war had to be fought. Their theme had not changed much since 1702, although it was overridden by the tack in 1705. When it reappeared in 1708, if only in muted volume, the only thing different about it was that it carried an oblique reference to (soon to be a flat charge of) war profiteering.

A fourth issue we have already alluded to in discussing the Pretender's attempted invasion of Scotland: the revolution of 1688 and the revolution settlement. It was spiritedly discussed by party propagandists apart from the invasion attempt, however. Always fundamental to men of the early eighteenth

22. *Rehearsal*, III, no. 16, May 28, 1708.

century, the issue appeared in every election of the period. And in every election whatever and however many the positions on immediate, concrete issues might be, there were only two on the revolution and revolution settlement. They were traditional Whig and Tory. The techniques and arguments with which they were presented remained the same. These had become conventional by the first general election of the reign and nothing substantially changed until the queen's death in 1714. Whigs charged that Tory principles were antithetical to the revolution settlement and the Protestant succession and tendentious to tyranny. Tories were not univocal in their views but had some stock arguments, for example, that passive obedience and nonresistance were not absolutely vital to Tory doctrines, that Whigs were traducing a gracious and merciful queen by talking about resistance, or that Tory principles were not treasonable or conducive to tyranny but natural and divinely ordained. The latter position was High Tory and Leslie argued it in 1708.

Defoe's *Review* in 1708 summarized the traditional Whig position—the position he always adopted, even when working for Harley:

> If you would have the Revolution damn'd for a cursed Rebellion ... If you will have a Sanction put upon all the Tyranny and Illegal Practices of the two Anti-Revolution Reigns ... If you would unsettle the Succession, and recognize the Right of King James III, *Jure Divino* ... and acknowledge the Settlement a Parliamentary Usurpation, and an Invasion of Right ... then Choose Tories and High-Flyers, and send them up to the House, that by their precipitant Follies they may truly represent your own.[23]

23. *Review*, v, no. 26, May 27, 1708; no. 27, May 29, 1708. Also the *Observator*, VIII, no. 23, May 1–5, 1708.

The *Rehearsal* answered for Tory ideology, citing history and biblical authority to prove that passive obedience, nonresistance, and divine right monarchy were part of natural law and divinely planned. Leslie argued at considerable length (even for him) that Whigs were incapable of maintaining order and tranquility because their principles led to violence and anarchy. By citing the events of the 1640s he tried to convince readers that, whatever their intentions, Whigs would again subvert the constitution and establish a commonwealth if they got into power.[24]

The last issue discussed in the election propaganda, the position of the church, is an anomalous issue for it was certainly not related to any of the important events which surrounded the election—the war, the invasion, and maladministration. The issue of the church had been in abeyance since the election of 1705 except during the debates over the union with Scotland when the High Flyers had warned that granting concessions to the Scottish Presbyterians would endanger the established church. But during the election of 1708 Tories did not introduce this question into their propaganda about the church. So traditional were their arguments that they could have been written for any election of the period. Their object, however, was twofold: they were not only concerned about the position of the church, but they were also attempting to arouse interest in an issue on which they felt their position was strong, an issue that would, they hoped, draw attention away from the Pretender's invasion. Leslie, for the Tories, always presumed that state and church were inextricably intertwined. If a person did not subscribe to the doctrines of the established church, he was not only antigovernment but basically antimonarchical as well.

24. *Rehearsal,* II, no. 42, March 3, 1708; no. 43, March 6, 1708; III, nos. 10, 12, 13, May 5, 12, 15, 1708.

Leslie, therefore, always said—and High Tories believed—that voters "ought not to chuse dissenters, who are profess'd adversaries; nor Lo-Church-Men, who are very indifferent friends; nor Whiggs, who care for no Church," and warned that "whoever votes for any such, has no great good will to the church or at best is very indifferent to her concerns."[25] Tory strategy was probably on the whole a wasted effort, considering how little influence this issue (and others for that matter) had on most actual contests.[26]

Writers who believed the traditional Whig views on a latitudinarian church answered the Tories, however, because any Tory charge that Whig ideology was irreligious and antichurch always drew a reply, regardless of how important other issues might be. The position of the church thus was a fundamental truth even to those who did not believe the church was in danger. Defoe and the writers of the *Observator* replied to Tory propaganda with the conventional accusations of High Tory intolerance, divisive fanaticism, and persecution. Electing High Tories, Defoe warned, would mean a repetition of such madness as the tack of 1705. "Their whole Practice has been a State-Lunacy, and you must be all Lunatick, if you choose them."[27] The *Observator* joined the *Review* on this issue inveighing against Tory persecuting zeal and calling for the election of men who would repeal the penal laws against Dissenters and the Sacramental Test.[28]

There were, then, incisively drawn party lines on such tra-

---

25. Ibid., nos. 14, 15, 16, May 19, 22, 26, 1708.

26. It is true, however, that the church as an issue did appear in some contests whereas the invasion attempt, an immediate concrete issue, did not. Does that make the church a more important issue than the invasion?

27. *Review*, v, no. 27, May 29, 1708.

28. *Observator*, VII, no. 22, April 28–May 1, 1708; no. 29, May 22–26, 1708.

ditional issues as the church, the revolution settlement and the Protestant succession, and the war. Conventional ideological party lines blurred almost indistinguishably on the remaining issues of maladministration and the Pretender's invasion. The phenomenon of ideological fluidity together with the political struggles occurring at Westminster injected an element of uncertainty into the elections, an element that had not been present since 1702 when public uncertainty about the policies of the new monarch and her government had allowed local issues to dominate the election contests. In 1708 neither those voters loyal to the government nor those hostile to it had a clear conception of what the national party issues were. The party organs were unreliable. The *Observator*, hitherto staunchly Whig, was defending Tories against the charge of Jacobitism and attacking a ministry it had supported in the last general election. And though the *Review* offered a well-reasoned, coherent defense of the ministry, local voters could not be certain that the outcome of the struggles at Westminster would permit the ministry to continue the policies advocated by Defoe. The High Tories were equally perplexed by the turn of events; their *Rehearsal* offered only general conventional advice that they defend the church and beware of republican Whigs.

Ideology did figure, as we have come to expect, in some of the county and larger borough elections. At Hereford, a large freeman borough, Thomas Foley, brother-in-law and close political associate of Robert Harley, kept his seat, despite some Jacobite opposition, because he had strong support from local churchmen.[29] In Hertfordshire, exulted one local Tory, the church party carried the election despite the opposition of the lord chancellor, who "was to advance the Whig's interest, leaving

29. H.M.C., Portland MSS, IV, 437, 483–487.

Westminster Hall for two or three days in the middle of term."[30] And at Durham the local schoolmaster saved Tory Thomas Conyers's seat for him by threatening his opposition that "damnation wd be their future lott, if they did not repent of such an heinous sin, as the very attempting to reject so true and trusty a member of the church."[31] Tory propagandists, we speculated earlier in the chapter, had hoped the issue of the church would distract attention from other issues. Perhaps at Durham, Hereford, and Hertfordshire it did, if not at any other places.

But in few of the freer constituencies was propaganda aimed at specific voters. London was one of the few. Most propaganda was available to that electorate anyway, but the *Observator* singled out city elections in an issue and pleaded with electors to choose men who would take the Whig side on all issues the journal had raised during the campaign, particularly on the issue of maladministration.[32] The results were not encouraging to those who believed the Whigs held a strong advantage on issues. There had been four Whigs returned from the city in 1705. In 1708 there were only three. The intention of the Junto was to continue opposition to the ministry through the general election in the hope of gaining extra strength to force Godolphin and Marlborough to give them cabinet posts. Their specific plan was to be sufficiently antiministerial on the concrete, immediate issues of the election to enable Whigs to win at the expense of the government but not to drive voters to the Tories. The plan failed; what the Junto did not want to

30. Great Britain, Historical Manuscripts Commission, Report on the MSS of the Earl of Downshire, I, pt. 2, 857–858. Cited in later notes as H.M.C., Downshire MSS.

31. Speck, "The House of Commons, 1702–1714," p. 383.

32. See the *Observator*, VII, no. 22, April 28–May 1, 1708.

happen did. If their propaganda had an impact on the election it was to encourage voters to turn to the right of the political spectrum and choose a new man, a Tory, and almost defeat the other Whig candidates. Defoe's bitter comment on the London election and Junto aims was that they had "turn'd their Backs upon their Friends, divided the Interest, voted for an Enthron'd Statue; and made the Office Parliament-Men."[33] The outcome was a portent of the strong anti-Whig election tide of 1710. Middlesex was another of the constituencies for which the *Observator* wrote specifically. One of the two returned incumbents was an independent Tory whose election may owe something to the miscalculated effect of the *Observator* or even to the antiministerialism of the High Tory *Honest Advice to the Electors,* but such an argument would have to be a tenuous one.

What were the election results in the counties and larger boroughs and what can be argued from them? In earlier general elections trends and patterns seem to have emerged more sharply in these constituencies than in the smaller, narrower ones. In 1708 the evidence is not complete. But where party affinities can be ascertained from biographical evidence, a pattern of changes does emerge, even if the sample available is small.[34] In twelve of the larger boroughs ten incumbent Tories were defeated and either Whigs or government sympathizers elected in their places. In the remaining four boroughs five seats changed in the other direction, London being one of the boroughs with two of the seats. Similar discernible changes in partisan affinities took place in eleven counties. Seven of the eleven changes were from Tory to Whig, governmental or local in-

33. *Review*, v, no. 21, May 15, 1708.

34. The biographical information comes from Cunnington, "The General Election of 1705"; Ransome, "The General Election of 1710"; and Walcott, *English Politics.*

terest; four were from Whig to Tory. Therefore, a national trend toward those who identified themselves as Whig or pro-government did appear more strongly in the counties and larger boroughs than among the national electoral structure. The nearly two-to-one margin of Whig victories there far exceeded the national percentage of gains, 13 percent, which Whig and proministerial M.P.'s made over Tories.[35] The cause of the increased percentages of gains in larger constituencies is not directly relatable to propaganda because we have not enough evidence that propaganda reached voters in those contests. We might speculate on the importance of ideology by restating a judgment about the election of 1702: The simple fact that stronger gains were registered in open constituencies than in controlled ones argues the importance of ideas and intangible factors induced by partisan literature, personal hard interests of politicians having less hold on such electorates. But that is speculation.

In most of the contests, however, voters and candidates, although generally aware that a strong tide of Whig sentiment was sweeping the country, turned their attention to local and more concrete issues so that the incidence of partisan ideology in local contests was not high even in the larger, freer constituencies. This turn in the elections materially aided the Tories; if they were weak and disorganized, their opponents were too preoccupied to take advantage of the situation. The absence of national issues in the local elections enabled the Tories to retain a modicum of their control in the constituencies. Harley, for example, had been active in the counties long before he ceased to be secretary of state and, despite his diminished po-

35. W. A. Speck calculates that Whigs gained 33 seats over their number in 1705, which was 250; Tories dropped 33 from 263 ("House of Commons, 1702–1714," pp. 418ff.).

litical influence, was able to marshal a significant number of followers in the new Parliament. He sought the aid of his old friend, William Penn, in obtaining the votes of the Quakers, and even made overtures to the Duke of Shrewsbury in an effort to secure his electoral influence.[36]

Harleyites were successful in Herefordshire, Derbyshire, Staffordshire, Yorkshire, Nottinghamshire, and in Wales, although they were unable to recover all the seats they had held in sunnier days. In Wales, always a Harley stronghold, Harley himself maintained his old seat at Radnor and followers secured one county seat each in Glamorgan and Radnor. The Harleyites numbered at least twelve in the new Parliament,[37] a tribute to Harley's political vitality during a period when it was commonly believed that his fortunes were at their lowest depths.

But these gains were not typical of Tory fortunes in the constituencies, for while the Harleyites were rather successful in getting themselves elected, the followers of such Tory leaders as the Earls of Nottingham and Rochester and Sir Edward Seymour were losing quite heavily. In the elections of 1705 the number of the followers of Rochester and Seymour had dropped from sixty-six to forty, but in the elections of 1708 this number dropped even lower, to twenty-nine.[38] Seats lost in 1705 in Lancashire, Westmorland, Gloucester, Huntingdon, Stafford-

36. See H.M.C., Portland MSS, IV, 437, 461; H.M.C., Bath MSS, I, 190–191; Great Britain, Historical Manuscripts Commission, Report on the MSS of the Duke of Buccleuch, Montagu House, Whitehall, p. 720. Cited in later notes as H.M.C., Buccleuch MSS.

37. This figure is based on Walcott's study of the Harleyites in the 1702 election in *English Politics*, pp. 225–226, and Great Britain, Parliament, House of Commons (Reports and Papers, Vol. LXIX, pts. 1 and 2), *Members of Parliament* (1878), passim. Cited in later notes as *Members of Parliament.*

38. This, too, is based on Wolcott's figures for the 1702 and 1705 elections and *Members of Parliament* for the 1708 election. See Walcott, pp. 60–66, 222–225, and *Members of Parliament* for the electoral interests of Rochester and Seymour in the 1708 elections.

shire, Somerset, Devon, and Cornwall could not be retaken in 1708. Seymour's once impressive "Western Empire" had deep fissures in its structure, and his once vaunted personal following of twenty-five had shrunk after the elections of 1708 were over to just half that size. Seymour himself, accustomed to being returned from Exeter, a large freeman borough, had to retreat to his pocket borough at Totnes to find a seat. The shadow of the Tory debacle of 1705 also hung over Rochester. Handicapped by the loss of his offices as in the elections of 1705, he could do nothing to prevent the defeat of his candidates at Westminster and Huntingdon, constituencies which had elected Rochesterites in 1702.

The Tory leader whose electoral interest suffered the heaviest loss, however, was the Earl of Nottingham. His allies, who had totaled fifty members in the Parliament of 1702 and had dropped to thirty-nine in the Parliament of 1705, numbered only nineteen after the elections of 1708.[39] In Kent and Norfolk, where Nottingham's candidates had done well in 1702, no seats were taken. And in Wales and Wiltshire, where friends had normally won in the past, only a handful were successful in 1708.

It is clear, then, that the Tories were losing the election, but who was winning it? The obvious answer would seem to be Whigs, but even a rather cursory examination of the election returns shows that the organized Whigs at least were scoring few victories. The Junto Whig lords had thought to do rather well in open constituencies by using a plan of limited opposition to the ministry. Things did not work out that way, nor did they in constituencies where the use of personal interest usually sufficed. Even the most formidable Junto electioneer, Lord Whar-

39. See Walcott, pp. 54–60, 219–221, and *Members of Parliament* for Nottingham's electoral interest and the 1708 elections.

ton, encountered unexpected reversals.[40] His interest extended the length of the nation, from Cumberland, Westmorland, and York in the north to Wiltshire in the south. Buckinghamshire, where Wharton's country seat lay, was the most important component of this interest. Wharton had been quite successful there in 1705; ten of his followers had secured seats. But in the election of 1708 this number slipped to eight, a surprising development since the Whigs were commonly believed to be winning the election. And in nearby Wiltshire, Calne, which was usually controlled by Wharton's friends, chose men not associated with any of the important Whig or Tory leaders. Wharton therefore was not uniformly successful in the elections. He had in fact done little to augment his parliamentary following, and his Junto allies could boast no better fortunes. In fact the Junto failed to return as many members as it had in the 1705 Parliament.[41] So if the election was a Whig victory it was not a Junto victory. Here and there we see evidence that political conditions had permitted and even encouraged local, primarily Whig politicians, who were not tied to the national party leaders, to seize control temporarily of such constituencies as Huntingdon, Wells, and Sudbury, Suffolk. Only through an alliance with the Scottish *Squadrone*[42] which had dominated

---

40. See Walcott, pp. 39–46, 229–232, and *Members of Parliament* for the Junto Lords' electoral interests and the elections of 1708.

41. Walcott, p. 150.

42. The *Squadrone Volante*, a party of Scottish peers and commoners, generally Whiggish in politics, which aligned itself with the Junto in Parliament. See Walcott, pp. 150–151.

Although the reader will note that this study is of *English*, not British, party propaganda, some explanation should be given about the omission of Scottish elections during Anne's reign, especially those of 1708, 1710, and 1713 after the establishment of the Union. The most important larger reason for omitting Scottish elections is the wide historical divergence between English and Scottish domestic politics. Attempting to study both English and Scottish elections and issues necessitates combining disparate political tradithe elections there and because through their superior organization they controlled the new Parliament was the Junto able successfully to complete its campaign to force the queen and the government to grant those concessions originally demanded during the winter session of 1707–1708.

The government had to meet those demands because its own gains during the election had not been substantial enough to permit it to operate without the Junto's bloc of votes. Godolphin's own private influence was exerted in the West Country where he had several pocket boroughs. His efforts were not without success, as one Cornish Tory correspondent attested by remarking to Harley: "these two last elections [1705 and 1708] have made us rather worse than better in this County."[43] But victories there and in the Cinque Ports and government-controlled boroughs were not enough. The government's inability to obtain a clear majority in the new House of Commons meant that the Junto had to be brought into the inner circle of government.

---

tions and electoral systems. Furthermore, extant political literature reveals that Scottish affairs exercised no major influences on English elections. Even in the 1708 election when presumably the Act of Union still alarmed those churchmen and Tories greatly concerned about the safety of the Church of England, there were only scant references to that event in certain pieces of Tory propaganda. And these references are not such as to warrant a consideration of the matter as an issue.

English propagandists did not often write for the Scottish elections, even after the Union. Such propaganda would have been virtually useless anyway because of the nature of Scottish politics. In addition to the limited base of the franchise there were other factors which denied the persuasive arts of the political writer any real success. The clannish influence predominated; politics to a degree unknown in England were a matter of personal loyalties. The chief of the clan himself decided the political disposition of the clan, that is, whether the clan was Jacobite or "on a Revolution foot" as G. M. Trevelyan put it. Even more important were the long-standing feuds between clans that had by Anne's reign already determined the political divisions of Scotland.

43. H.M.C., Portland MSS, IV, 489–490, George Granville to Harley, May 20, 1708.

[*The General Election of 1708*]

The election of 1708 was the testing time of the ministerial-Whig alliance and bears the appropriate marks of such a period. Neither the election itself nor the propaganda campaign preceding it was conducted wholly along traditional party lines. Because Anne detested the Junto, the government attempted to maintain its political integrity by rallying the nation to its support and the defense of its policies. It failed. The Junto lords themselves may not have won a clear majority in the new Parliament, but other Whigs who had come in by a fair-sized margin over Tories would listen to the Junto before they would the government. The Junto would get its way. In this power struggle the Tories, though slowly and inevitably driven back together by the turn of events, were only bystanders without the means or will for effective political action. They were obviously marking time until more propitious circumstances should permit their resurgence. The opportunity came in 1710 in the form of the Sacheverell affair.

The General Election of 1710

IV The general election of 1710, even more than that of 1705, demonstrates the strength of ideology in the functioning of the electoral system of Queen Anne's reign. Prior to 1710, only in the general election of 1705 had partisan issues exercised a strong discernible influence on elections. The election of 1702 was a time of experimentation and testing of ideological differences, although political circumstances worked to keep ideology out of most contests. The election of 1705 provides considerable evidence that ideological issues did matter. Ideology as an electoral determinant reached its nadir in the election of 1708. But 1710 as a case study of propaganda in elections is unique in the degree to which ideology's electoral significance overshadows local personal interests.[1] It is also unique in the quality of partisan passions and the quantity of election propaganda produced. Several circumstances blended to produce such an election. The continuing struggles of Tory, Whig, and ministerial leaders over control of the government and the trial of Dr. Henry Sacheverell were of immediate importance. Underlying these was public weariness of the war which exacerbated political and religious tensions.

Once the Junto had forced its way into the Godolphin ministry, it began to exert a dominant influence on policy-making, particularly toward continuing the war until the French re-

---

1. Two articles have been written about this election by Mary Ransome, "The Press in the General Election of 1710," pp. 209–221, and "Church and Dissent in the Election of 1710," pp. 76–89. There is also an article by W. T. Morgan, "An Eighteenth-Century Election in England," pp. 585–604.

nounced the Bourbon claim to Spain. Through 1709 and 1710, even though the war did not turn conclusively one way or the other, and despite mounting evidence of public discontent, the government kept its faith that the French will would break. But the Duke of Shrewsbury wondered how long the British will would last: "it is evident so many circumstances from at home as well as from abroad make peace desirable, that if the nation could see how they might have a good one, it is my opinion they would be very uneasy till they had it."[2]

Meanwhile, Robert Harley, out of power, was contemplating ways of getting back into power. One of the ways was to unite the Tories once again. The entente made in the fall of 1708 was expedient and uneasy because High Tories did not think Harley was really a Tory (and they were correct); Harley remembered their extremism and knew he could not count on their steady support.[3] The queen was the key to Harley's plans because only she could change cabinets. But she feared a repetition of Harley's ignominious failure to form a government in 1708, so she waited until the Sacheverell trial backfired against Godolphin and the Whigs and gave her the sign she wanted to bring Harley in. The ministry had not planned a quiet trial for Dr. Henry Sacheverell, but the outcome was far beyond their aims and anything but their intention.[4] They wanted to make an example of Sacheverell, who had always been the bête noir of Whigs because of a sermon he delivered on Guy Fawkes Day 1709, defending the doctrine of absolute nonresistance, assailing the idea of toleration, warning of the church's imminent dan-

2. H.M.C., Bath MSS, I, 197, Shrewsbury to Harley, November 3, 1709.

3. For some of the High Tory opinions about Harley, see H.M.C., Portland MSS, IV, 574–575, and James J. Cartwright, ed., *The Wentworth Papers, 1705–1739* (1883), p. 152.

4. See Abbie Scudi, *The Sacheverell Affair* (1939), for the fullest account of the whole incident.

ger, and insinuating that the royal ministers were conniving at its destruction. The verdict was not unexpected. The Whigs had more votes in the House of Lords than did Tories. What the government had not counted on was the vast public outpouring of sympathy and support for Sacheverell. The queen herself on coming to and going from the trial was deafened by cries of "God bless your Majesty. We hope your Majesty is for Dr. Sacheverell."[5] That convinced her that she could turn out the Godolphin government which she did in the summer of 1710.[6]

It was not certain that a new ministry would mean the calling of a new Parliament. Harley preferred not to have the country go to the polls. He hoped instead to secure the support of key Whig leaders—including the Junto lord Halifax—for the new government and to avoid certain High Tory success in a frenzied, general election. Harley still hoped to implement the ideas of political moderation and consensus; High Tory extremism would defeat his aims and he did not want a majority of Tories at his back.[7] By September, however, Harley, not having gotten sufficient Whig support (ideological polarization preventing it), had reluctantly become convinced that the only way he could get a parliamentary majority was to go to the polls.

The issuance of writs for new elections did not precipitate the massive flow of propaganda of 1710. Even before Sacheverell's trial ended a prodigious amount of paper had been consumed

---

5. Ibid., p. 1.

6. For background on the change of ministries see W. T. Morgan, "The Ministerial Revolution of 1710 in England," pp. 184–210.

7. Harley's memorandum of May 20, 1710, expressed his aim of grafting "the Whigs on the bulk of the Church Party" (Holmes, *British Politics*, p. 380). Jonathan Swift wrote "I have been told, that Mr. Harley himself would not let the Tories be too numerous, for fear they should be insolent, and kick against him." (*Journal to Stella*, I, 44).

in arguments about it. The general election by itself did not call forth the new journals of 1710 or the ideological positions they assumed either. The *Examiner*, *Moderator*, *Whig–Examiner*, and *Medley* had purposes which carried them beyond the electoral contests. The year 1710 marked the beginning of the most intensely partisan years of Anne's reign. Seriousness in the use of political literature and the articulation of ideological differences was unmatched in the earlier years, partisan though they were, and was stimulated by polarization on the war, the succession question, and religion. But the election occurred at the commencement of that phase and perhaps gave it impetus since the task of helping shape the composition of the new House of Commons was the immediate one writers had.

No politician had a larger coterie of writers than Harley, who sought penmen for specific and different purposes.[8] Secretly Harley was worried that the High Tories would muster such electoral strength from the Sacheverell affair that he could not manage them. He could not afford to quarrel publicly with them on the eve of elections, however, so if he were to do anything against them it would have to be done covertly. Daniel Defoe was capable of that kind of responsibility and he believed in Harley's ideas. He had managed an anti-Tacker campaign in 1705 and wanted to work for Harley again, as he said in a letter dated July, 1710.[9] Harley began to use him, as he had in 1705, to conduct a moderation and consensus campaign designed to weaken the influence of High Tories and to rally what Whig support he could for the new ministry. The two aims were interrelated. However, convincing Whigs that the new ministry

8. Stevens, *Party Politics*, chaps. 3, 4, and 5 discuss Harley's interest in writers in 1710.

9. See H.M.C., Portland MSS, IV, 550–553, for Defoe's letters in July to Harley.

deserved their support was Defoe's contribution to the issue of the change of ministries which we shall discuss later. Discrediting High Toryism and diminishing popular enthusiasm for Sacheverell was the facet of the moderation campaign aimed at the issue of the Sacheverell affair.

In the *Review* and in various pamphlets Defoe hammered on a single theme: High Church principles were inconsistent with the administration of government. Government depended on policies of moderation and prudence; High Churchmen thrived on violence. Having them in control would mean having a perpetual uproar, and it would mean a return of the Pretender, whom Sacheverell and the High Tories by their principles were working to restore.[10] If you vote for such, "you set Fire to your own Houses, you Undermine your own Privileges, you Pull Down your Protestant Queen, you say Backward all your Laws of Liberty, you brand your Deliverer, King William, for an Usurper, and make a Witches Prayer of the Revolution."[11] Neither the queen nor the ministry wanted to see extremists bent on revenge elected to the new Commons. They wanted and the country needed sober moderate men to help carry on the government.

If such propaganda succeeded it would serve not to prevent a Tory victory, nor even a High Tory one, but to make such a victory a marginal one. The impact of moderation literature is difficult to assess. Any influence Defoe's writings—and those of any others doing the same service for the new ministry—

10. See the *Review*, VII, no. 66 and following numbers. Defoe also wrote *A New Test of the Sence of the Nation* (1710) on the same theme. The popular *Faults on Both Sides* (1710), attributed to Harley himself, also urged a policy of moderation, and called for electors to return men "without any consideration of their party." The authorship is discussed in Ransome, "The Press in the General Election of 1710," pp. 214–215, n. 33.

11. *A Word Against a New Election* (1710).

might have had could be registered in Whig victories as well as in moderate Tory ones, if some people did indeed become alarmed at High Tory extremism and vote against it. But even if we could identify the reasons for separate Whig and moderate Tory successes the sum of such successes would still not have mattered in the final election results. So a general judgment about the moderation campaign would have to be that it did not accomplish its purposes any more than did the vast amounts of Whig-inspired literature on the Sacheverell affair.

Much of the Whig literature came from anonymous penmen. It was unified by the core of traditional Whig ideology on the revolution, a commitment to the right to resistance against royal tyranny and to the revolution settlement, and by a repertoire of traditional techniques which equated Toryism with a French and popish take-over. Although some of the partisan pieces do seem to have been commissioned, these ideas were as fundamental for real Whigs as religious dogma. Party leaders did not have to instigate their written defense, especially when Sacheverell had stirred up so many Whigs. There were poems denouncing Sacheverell as a "proud and saucy Levite" and warning electors of the dangers that "pious Fraud and Passive Popish Prate"[12] posed to their lands and liberties. There was also doggerel for street mobs and Whig clubs to sing:

> You pinnacle-flyers, where would you advance?
> What, would ye be bringing of Perkin from France?
> Instead of a bowl fill'd up to the brim,
> A halter for those that would bring Perkin in![13]

---

12. *The Tacking Club; or a Satyr on Dr. Sacheverell and his Bulleys* (1710) and *Honest Clodd's Advice to his Countrymen* (1710).

13. Thomas Wright, *Caricature History of the Georges; Or Annals of the House of Hanover* (1868), p. 6.

There were, as well, dozens of more sober persuasive works. Several of them were from the pen of Benjamin Hoadly, whose Whiggism was distinguished in attacks on High Tory principles even before the Sacheverell trial and who was chaplain to the wealthy Whig Duke of Bedford, relative of one of the Junto lords, Orford.[14] Hoadly's *Serious Advice to the Good People of England* assured the voters that the Whigs had used "their greatest zeal to prove you to be Freemen, and not Slaves" and described the High Tories as those "whose Principles naturally draw you back to Egyptian Darkness and Slavery." In a similar vein his *Letter of Advice to the Freeholders of England* stated: "The Whigs . . . declare you to be a Free People, invested with a Right to defend that Freedom. The Tories either declare you to be no better than slaves; or, at least, profess that you have no more Right to defend yourselves . . . than the greatest Slaves in the World have." Still classically Whig but closer perhaps in origin to the Junto was the short-lived *Whig-Examiner*, edited and written in the main by Joseph Addison, who had served as the Earl of Wharton's chief secretary in Ireland until just before the elections.[15] Addison dismissed Sacheverell's—and High Tory—doctrines as "the Sublime in Nonsense," although he took up one issue to object vehemently to nonresistance and passive obedience as suitable for "Turks and Indians, who have no Laws above the Will of a Grand Signior or a Mogul."[16]

---

14. See the article in *Dictionary of National Biography*, IX, 910–915. I have followed Morgan, *Bibliography of British History* in attributing the pamphlets discussed in the text to Hoadly.

15. On Addison and the *Whig-Examiner* see Bertrand A. Goldgar, *The Curse of Party: Swift's Relations with Addison and Steele* (1961), pp. 66–67.

16. *Whig-Examiner*, nos. 4, 5, October 5, 12, 1710. Similar were the *Observator*, IX, no. 77, October 11, 1710, and the *Medley*, nos. 3, 4, October

For their part High Tories, apparently having discovered during the trial the strength of the fear that the church was indeed threatened, concentrated on making the church, and the monarchy, seem more endangered by Whiggism instead of arguing the compatibility of Tory doctrines and the revolution settlement. They did not duck Whig charges of Jacobitism, a French take-over, and popery. They did not face them squarely either. They could not: what their hearts told them to prefer, the Act of Settlement denied. Among the reams of propaganda on the trial (none of which, it might be noted in passing, is clearly associable with High Tory leaders), the pattern was to extol the queen and profess being shocked that Whigs could talk about resistance while being governed by "so excellent a princess."[17] A new journal, the *Moderator*, did take on the job of explaining nonresistance and passive obedience and attacking Whig political theories.[18] Its arguments were sometimes ingenious, but they added nothing substantially to what Charles Leslie had expounded in the *Rehearsal* until its demise in 1709. The tone was defensive, as if in overreaction, and as if the writers were working on their own consciences as well as trying to change Whig ones.

Sacheverell's national popularity was already established by the time of the elections. So too was the effectiveness of the cry, "The Church in Danger!" Tories exploited both. They produced doggerel to match the Whigs':

16, 23, 1710 (begun by Arthur Maynwaring on October 15, doubtless with Junto backing). Also Maynwaring's *Four Letters to a Friend in North Britain* (1710).

17. Ransome, "The Press in the General Election of 1710," p. 214.

18. See, for instance, no. 11, June 23, 1710; no. 23, August 4, 1710; no. 40, October 2, 1710.

Ye Whigs and Dissenter, what would ye have done?
Ne'er think of restoring your old '41.
Then fill up a bowl, fill it up to the brim;
Here's a health to all those whom the Church do esteem!

. . . .

While the Phoenix stands up, and the Bow bells do ring,
Here's a health to Sachev'rell, and God bless the Queen![19]

To Whig poems they opposed their own which likened the impeachment before the House of Lords to Charles I's trial and declared Sacheverell worthy of "a mitre here, a glorious crown in Heaven."[20] Longer pieces focused on the specter of the 1640s which Whigs—sons of the "vile Cut-throats of Forty eight"[21]—would make the country relive. This was not a new device; Leslie and other Tory writers had made use of it in every earlier election. Tories obviously were closed-minded when it came to the possibility of Whig loyalty. They really thought that moderation, toleration, and occasional conformity were only ruses to destroy the church and the monarchy and that the only hope was to "Chuse . . . Sound, Sober, Pious, and Loyal Members of the Church of England."[22]

A significant part of the aftermath of the Sacheverell trial had been the ministerial shuffle of the summer of 1710.[23] That became a partisan issue: Whigs predicted the ills the change of ministers would bring and Tories, both the hot ones and the

19. Wright, pp. 5–6.

20. Ransome, "The Press in the General Election of 1710," p. 212.

21. *Moderator*, no. 23, August 4, 1710.

22. *This is the Time: or Serious Advice . . . Concerning the Election of Members of Parliament* (1710). See also *Bodkins and Thimbles: or 1645 Against 1710* (1710); *Jack Presbyter's Downfal* (1710); *The Calamity of the Church of England* (1710).

23. See note 6 above.

Harleyite ones uniting on this point, defended the change. One of Defoe's jobs was to make the Harley ministry look attractive to Whigs, which would also help to balance High Tory strength, Defoe's other assignment. He repeated the nonideological appeal of 1705: the important thing was not who governed but how they governed. If the new ministers governed well, it was imperative that "all honest Men join with them, never enquiring into the Principle from which they Act."[24] And they would govern well. They were committed to principles of moderation and prudence; they would be, Defoe said, "Whiggs in Practice."[25] Even Whig self-interest lay in standing behind the government, because if Harley could not muster support from Whig financiers, the ministry's credit would be hurt and the repercussions would envelop everyone.[26] There was a certain species of logic in this, but how much of it did Harley believe Whigs would accept? Almost none of the Whig leaders had responded to his efforts earlier to avoid elections. He had little reason to think many others would be swayed by Defoe, but he apparently thought the effort to sway them worthwhile.

Actually there were two facets of the ministerial campaign to justify the change of ministries to voters. Besides Defoe's writings, which Harley himself secretly was influencing, there was an openly proministerial point of view represented by the new journal, the *Examiner*. Guided by Henry St. John, the paper was group-written by Francis Atterbury, William King, and

---

24. *Review*, VII, no. 62.

25. Ibid., VII, nos. 65, 81.

26. Defoe's *Essay Upon Public Credit* (1710) was aimed at the question of credit. He mentions it in a letter to Harley in August: H.M.C., Portland MSS, IV, 585. Richard I. Cook, *Jonathan Swift as a Tory Pamphleteer* (1967), pp. 103ff., has an interesting analysis of Defoe's use of rhetoric for a commercial audience.

St. John himself the first few weeks after it began, August 3. The new journal was to show the merits of the new ministry and blacken the deeds of the old one, especially those of the Junto, and specifically the conduct of the war.[27] Its appearance with Harley's knowledge and financial support is puzzling in a sense because Harley presumably deplored aggressive partisanship such as the *Examiner* displayed. St. John did not share Harley's predilection for consensus, and his influence over the paper was strong, stronger probably than Harley's. But it is Harley's mind and intentions which supply the key. Given to compromising and vacillating and experimenting, Harley probably saw the *Examiner* as another straw in the wind, along with the *Review*, but one whose direction was much less uncertain. Very few of his extremists would not like the paper; it would make them less unhappy about having a Tory ministry without a zealous Tory leader. It could also sound out ways of reversing the policies of the old ministry and working toward new ones, particularly on the war.

Like Defoe's *Review*, the paper called for all honest men to join in support of the new government, but its attitude toward the old ministers, especially the Junto, was not reconciliatory. Whig imputations of Jacobitism and Francophilia to Harley and his colleagues stung Tories. So did the charges, widely repeated by Whigs, that the dissolution of the old Parliament had been an attempt, engineered from France, to scatter resolute men,[28] and the questioning of how safe public credit was

---

27. See Stevens, chap. 3, for the *Examiner*. Swift did not begin to write for the journal until November 2 when the elections were finished.

28. Charges of Jacobitism and the French influence, for instance, were made by the pamphlet, *Letter from Monsieur Pettecum to Monsieur Buys* (1710), written by an anonymous Whig.

in Tory care. Issues of the *Examiner*'s first two months dealt with the dissolving of Parliament primarily because the people wanted a new one and not because the French intrigued to get a more pliable one, with the turning out of Godolphin and the Whigs because they governed for their own interests instead of the queen's, and with the superior qualities of the new ministers, men fully as capable as the old ones and honest besides.[29] St. John himself struck back hardest at the Whigs in his *Letter to the Examiner* released in August.[30] He called them an "arbitrary Junto" who "would rather overturn the Chariot of Government than lose their place in it." He named the Duchess of Marlborough an "insolent woman" who "tried to make a slave of Her [the queen] in her Bedchamber." Those deeds, he thought, had really made the French king happy.

Whigs did raise questions of Jacobitism and French influence about the change of governments and the dissolution of Parliament.[31] What they said, mostly, was that Tories did not have the ability to govern. "Is it not a great pity, that so noble a vessel should be trusted in a storm with those pilots, that never could steer well, when out of one?"[32] Even "the French King," said the *Observator*, "knows their want of Ability from dear-bought Experience: for when that Faction had all the Power, and King Charles and the Duke of York at their head, he was forc'd to

---

29. See, for example, *Examiner*, nos. 1, 2, 3, 4, August 3–24, 1710. Also *Reasons for a Total Change of a Certain M——* (1710), *Letter from a Foreign Minister in England to Monsieur Pettecum* (1710), and the *Moderator*, no. 20, July 24, 1710, repeated the themes.

30. See H.M.C., Portland MSS, VII, 16, for a reference to the circulation of this pamphlet through the country.

31. As in Hoadly's *The French King's Thanks to the Tories of Great Britain* (1710).

32. *Seldom Comes a Better* (1710). Also *A Dialogue Betwixt Whig and Tory* (1710). Both pamphlets were anonymously written.

supply them with Pensions, as occasion requir'd."[33] The fall in stock values and in the government's credit, said the *Medley* (begun for the Junto by Arthur Maynwaring to oppose the *Examiner*) was proof that the country did not have faith in the new government.[34] And Benjamin Hoadly wondered what the nation would do without "Whig zeal and money."[35]

Whig propagandists also tried to make voters apprehensive about how Tories would conduct the war, somewhat as they and Defoe had tried to do in 1705 and 1708, forgetting or desperately ignoring the public weariness of the war by 1710. The Sacheverell furor, according to Benjamin Hoadly, was a ruse to turn attention away from the war and help the French recoup. It had worked, he said; the French were ready to fight on.[36] Tories would make peace immediately, said another writer, although "it is not yet time to conclude a peace, except we should suffer ourselves to be deluded into such a one, as would in all probability entail upon us greater miseries than those we have hitherto undergone."[37] "Whig-money and a Whig-administration," Hoadly hoped the electors would remember, had been committed to a policy of lasting peace which could only be won on the battlefield, not by offering concessions and entreating the French to negotiate. Tories by way of contrast had not wanted to declare war and had never really supported it.[38]

---

33. *Observator*, IX, no. 54, July 22, 1710. Also, Maynwaring's *Four Letters to a Friend* and Hoadly's *The Election Dialogue . . . , Concerning the Choice of Good Members for the Next Parliament* (1710).

34. *Medley*, no. 5, October 30, 1710. Maynwaring was to get "£100 down, and £100 a year as long as the paper continued" from his sponsors but apparently did not. On the journal see Stevens, pp. 72–73.

35. *A Letter of Advice to the Freeholders of England* (1710).

36. See ibid., *The Election Dialogue* and *The French King's Thanks.*

37. *Considerations on Peace and War* (1710), written anonymously.

38. *The Election Dialogue.*

The ministry's writers in reply offered no new policy on the war. The ministry had no definite policy. But for electoral purposes, since Whigs could no longer count on enthusiasm for the war as an asset, it was sufficient to say that peace with France was essential. The Whig ministry had been an obstacle to attaining this peace, although the new ministry, they hastily added, would not end the war before certain aims had been achieved or reduce the pressure on France. The *Examiner* was again the medium for the message. The French would find no reason to welcome a Tory ministry and majority in Parliament.[39] The new Parliament would not be weakened by factionalism and would produce better results than the old one: "France will soon lay aside her Artifices and Amusements, and in good earnest sue for Peace when she has no longer any Prospect of dividing us by continuing the War."[40] St. John's *Letter to the Examiner* explicitly attacked the Junto and the whole concept of the Continental land war against France which the Godolphin government had made its policy and followed since the beginning of the reign. That concept had been attacked as early as the 1702 election by Tories, but from 1710 the attacks emphasized that the military strategy of the concept was far less important to Whigs than the financial gains it brought by prolonging the war. St. John's conclusion was that until the Whig policies were ended "Britain may expect to remain exhausted of Men and Money, to see her Trade divided amongst her Neighbours, her Revenues anticipated even to future Generations, and to have this only Glory left Her, that She has proved a Farm to the Bank, a Province to Holland, and a Jest to the whole World." The *Examiner*, later

39. *Examiner*, no. 2, August 10, 1710.
40. Ibid., nos. 1, 3, August 3, 17, 1710.

in August, indicted "Ministers who are not for taking a good Peace when they can have it . . . who get by the War, and therefore desire to have it prolonged."[41] And in its instructions to voters it urged the election of men "who would push on the War with the utmost Vigor, in order to end it by a safe and speedy Peace."[42] "Choose those," it appealed, "who love their own Countrymen better than any Foreigner whatsoever; and would neither be enslav'd by the French, nor bubbled by any other Nation."[43]

In 1710 the *Examiner* was being read by electors as far away from London as Yorkshire. So were the *Observator* and *Review*,[44] and pamphlets were written for specific contests elsewhere to make ideology the test for choosing candidates. Was ideology the test? What influence generally did issues have? Evidence strongly suggests that ideology was indeed the test, that evidence being the electoral trend in those constituencies which we have judged most responsive to issues and propaganda—the universities, the more democratic boroughs, and the shires. Of the Tories' 99 new seats in the new House of Commons at least 64 were from the counties, the universities, and larger freeman and scot-and-lot boroughs. Those constituencies were not subject to decisive influence from the electoral interests of politicians.[45] There were at least 87 such constituencies returning 176 members to the House of Commons. So the proportion of new Tory seats to the total was 36 percent. Among

41. Ibid., no. 3, August 17, 1710.

42. Ibid., no. 10, October 5, 1710.

43. Ibid., no. 9, September 28, 1710.

44. Cook, *Jonathan Swift*, pp. 29–30.

45. I calculate this number from the biographical work done by Cunnington, "The General Election of 1705"; Ransome, "The General Election of 1710"; and the tabulation of election results by Speck, "The House of Commons, 1702–1714," pp. 418ff.

the rest of the constituencies which returned 313, the proportion of new Tory seats was 11 percent. Figuring another way to determine where the new Tory seats came from by type of constituency, we find that approximately 65 percent of them came from the freer and more issue-conscious constituencies.

Next we need to determine which issues were electorally significant, or which issues the constituencies seemed to be most conscious of. The answer could be given statistically on the Sacheverell case, which seemed to be very significant to people, if we could tally the M.P.'s who voted for and against the impeachment of Sacheverell and see how they did in contests. Unfortunately Commons did not vote directly on the impeachment, and the division lists on issues indirectly related to the trial are so ridden with discrepancies that an accurate tally of pro- and anti-Sacheverellites is not possible. So we are reduced to saying that in most of the contests where issues were involved the trial was the paramount issue.

Sacheverell himself made what amounted to an electoral tour in the summer on the way to a benefice in North Wales. He was accused of "parading around the country to influence the elections" and admitted that he would use his influence "to return such members to Parliament, as Favour the Church Establishment."[46] At virtually every town on his route officials, neighboring gentry and townsmen in large numbers met him, although his approach frequently created factionalism between those who wanted to entertain and those who wanted to ignore him.[47] Bridgnorth and Oxford City gave him lavish receptions, particularly Oxford to which he was "welcomed home" by Rowney, M.P., for the city.[48] When the election writs went out

46. See Scudi, p. 131.
47. Ibid., pp. 129ff.
48. H.M.C., Portland MSS, IV, 550.

the Sacheverell case became a test for candidates in many elections, in Norfolk, Yorkshire, Westmorland, Derby, Kent, Shropshire, Cambridgeshire, Cornwall, at Dorchester, Newcastle-upon-Tyne, Bridgnorth, Gloucester City, Chester, Bristol, and Newcastle-under-Lyme, to mention those for which evidence is available.[49]

Newcastle-upon-Tyne's election, for instance, turned upon the incumbent's opposition to Sacheverell.[50] Both members were Whigs. One had previously sat for three consecutive parliaments. Tories used a portrait of the doctor as their standard, carrying it "about the streets bedecked with laurels etc, which the people followed huzzaing to it." To distinguish themselves the local Tories "had red and blue favours in their hats with this motto in letters of gold, vizt.: for the Queen and Church. B. W." When Blackett and Wrightson (for whom the initials stood) won, the tumult continued in the streets:

> The streets rung loud, God Bless the Queen,
> And loudly we did speak it;
> The like this town had never seen,
> For Wrightson and for Blackett.

One statistical index of the issue's significance was the fate of the managers of the trial. Only ten of the twenty could find seats in the new Parliament. William Thompson at Ipswich

49. For elections not cited in the text, see Holmes, *British Politics*, p. 38, n. *; Speck, "The House of Commons, 1702–1714," pp. 394, 402, 410–411; Ransome, "The General Election of 1710," pp. 69–70, 114–115; J. W. F. Hill, ed., *The Letters and Papers of the Banks Family of Revesby Abbey, 1704–1760* (1952), p. 13; John Latimer, *The Annals of Bristol in the Eighteenth Century* (1893), pp. 85–86; H.M.C., Cowper MSS, III, 84–91.

50. See Speck, "The House of Commons, 1702–1714," pp. 392, 394, on the Newcastle election.

And groans beneath the Weight of Misery
We by a happier Fortune, are secure
From all those Ills which other Realms endure
No Hostile Foes our happy Lands invade
Nor has the Plague a devastation made
But though, as yet, we're freed from Forreign Wars
Brittania sinks by Her Intestine Jars
And ev'ry where such Gross Distinctions reign
As quite destroy that Peace we seek to gain;
Factions and Feuds do still amongst us rise
As angry Clouds obscure serener Skies
Yet now we hope much happier days to See
Since You our Representatives must be;
When such as You defend Britiania's cause
Protect our City and its Ancient Laws
The Church must flourish and the Nation be
Blest with that Ancient English Liberty
Which our Forefathers breasts at first inspir'd
And with a Noble British Spirit fir'd

And after all a Scrutiny demand
Yet even then You their Endeavours crost
And gain'd more by it than themselves had lost;
Were I to wish and cou'd my wish obtain
It shou'd be this (nor would I wish in vain)
That all our Representatives might be
Noted like You for their Integrity
Like Withers wise, Wealthy like Hoar & grave
Like Newland gen'rous & like Cass most brave;
Then wou'd ye Church for ever stand secur'd
From all those Blasts She has so long endur'd
And Factious Feuds that now her Ease disdain
Wou'd then oppose Her growing Pow'r in vain
The World shall Eccho wth Brittannia's Fame
Whilst distant Nations strive t'inscribe Her Name
And Europe shall with one Consent Aspire
To sing that Peace which such as you inspire.

1710

Printed for Wm. Pennok at a Picture Shop
in Panyer Alley in Paternoster Row, Price 1d

Whilst Europe's foes in wild Confusion lie   Though factious foes in vain yr Choice withstand

The Fourth Part of
Vulgus Britannicus:
OR, THE
Britiſh HUDIBRAS.

In Two *CANTOS*:

On the Coffee-Houſe Mob, or Debates *Pro*, and *Con*, on the Times.

A Character of ſeveral Sorts of *Whigs*, and *Falſe Brethren*, that are Enemies to the *Church*.

On the *Paper-War* betwixt *High* and *Low-Church*.

The *Loyal Engliſhman's* Prayer for the *Queen* and *Church*.

Written by the Author of the *London Spy*.

LONDON

Printed: and Sold by JAMES WOODWARD, in St. *Chriſtopher's* Church-Yard, near the *Royal Exchange*; and JOHN MORPHEW, near *Stationers-Hall*. M DCCX.

and Thomas Lord Coningsby at Leominster were among the ten who could not. At least seven apparently thought it useless to stand because of their notoriety. Six were returned by their old constituencies, although one had his election strongly contested and a petition filed against him. The other four had to go elsewhere for seats.[51] Robert Walpole, one of those who was reelected, stood for one of the county seats in Norfolk in addition to Castle Rising and King's Lynn. But county Tories singled him out both for his efforts against Sacheverell and his Whiggism. They "had Dr. Sacheverell's picture carryed before them & the cry was No Manager, No Scaffolder; but that was not all, for they pelted Mr. Walpole with dirt and stones & drove him out of his tent spoiling his fine lac't coat which they told him came out of the Trea^{ry}." Because Castle Rising and King's Lynn both elected Walpole, who chose to sit for the latter, he was luckier, even with the physical abuse, than most other managers and most other Whigs in Norfolk. The ten Whig seats from Norfolk in the old Parliament dropped to three in 1710.[52]

As might be expected London electors knew what all the issues were, and candidates usually seemed to feel that they had to take positions on the issues. Both sides wanted to win the four seats of the City for the symbolic effect of such a victory more than for the four places themselves. Five days before the election the *Observator* printed extensive directions to the electors on choosing candidates, asking them to put to the candidates twelve questions which summed up the Whig side on all the issues argued during the preceding months.[53] The *Supplement*, written by Abel Roper for the ministry, replied on the

51. Ransome, "The General Election of 1710," pp. 61–63.
52. For Walpole's elections and Norfolk see Holmes, *British Politics*, p. 231.
53. *Observator*, IX, nos. 75–76, October 4, 7, 1710.

day the poll opened, drawing together a consensus of Tory views which would please both moderate and High Tories and asking electors to give their votes to the four Tory candidates

> who are qualify'd for that high trust . . . by their affection to the Protestant Succession settled by Parliament in the illustrious House of Hanover; by their unalterable desire to live under a limited monarchy, without invading the just prerogatives of the Crown, or betraying the rights of the subject; by their zeal for the establish'd Church, without any tincture of popery or bigottry; by their tender regard to the indulgence granted to consciences truly scrupulous, without being a tool to lift up any one denomination of dissenters to be able to overcome all the rest, and monarchy and the Church too . . . and being independent of the Court, their debates, votes and resolutions will be free, and themselves without fears for the Old Ministry, or how their behaviour will be taken by the new . . . and lastly, who have not entertain'd such vast hopes of profit from the continuation of the war, as to remain wholly unconcern'd for general peace. . . .[54]

The upshot was that all four Tories won. Three of them won new seats in an election marked by mob abuse of Whig voters and candidates, one of whom was lord mayor of the City.[55]

Such actions and their reminder that many things produced election results lead us to the next query. How many victories did propaganda win or, to put the question another way, did partisan literature mold opinion so that it contributed decisively to the large Tory majority? We have identified the electoral trend in the freer constituencies, which strongly suggests, but

---

54. *Supplement*, October 9, 1710. See Hanson, *Government and the Press*, pp. 97–100, for Harley's control over the *Post Boy* and *Supplement*. The *Moderator*, no. 40, October 2, 1710, printed a similar appeal.

55. See W. T. Morgan, "An Eighteenth Century Election," pp. 594–595; H.M.C., Portland MSS, IV, 619.

only suggests, that ideology from some sources made a difference in those elections. But undoubtedly some of the ideology was a residue of earlier elections and partisan bickering. The Cheshire election indicates that issues lived from one election to succeeding ones. When High Tories won, people shouted, "Up with the Tackers," suggesting that they were feeling in some measure the passions of 1705 as well as those of 1710.[56] Miss Ransome thought that in 1710 "propaganda was the only force of really vital importance,"[57] notwithstanding other influences, including private and government patronage. The Sacheverell affair instigated strong party feelings about other issues and propaganda intensified and spread the partisanship. But her judgment was not based on a minute study of the force of propaganda in every contest because the data does not exist. Not even a satisfactorily representative sample has survived to give us a statistical analysis of the molding influence of propaganda on public opinion.

Some things we can say about the molding influence of propaganda in 1710. Partisan literature provided much of the information most voters had about issues. Gentlemen in the provinces had their correspondents in London who told them what was happening with Sacheverell, the ministry, and the war. But partisan newspapers and pamphlets gave more information regularly which helped to shape opinion, and that literature also keyed this information into partisan traditions. Whig and Tory publications broadened the impeachment of Sacheverell to symbolize traditional views on the safety of the church and the revolution settlement and wrote the change in governments into larger proportions embracing the disposition of the war, French subversion, and domestic security.

56. Ransome, "Church and Dissent," p. 78.
57. Ransome, "The General Election of 1710," p. 203.

The propaganda of 1710 did not transform totally unconcerned people into frenzied partisans. Rather it intensified partisanship by inflating some pre-existing and deep feelings about the church, the monarchy, the revolution of 1688, and the war and reflecting what those for whom it was written wanted and expected to hear. Both sides produced primarily that kind of propaganda which was visceral in its appeal rather than intellectual, and most effective not for winning new votes or supporters from the opposition but for persuading nominal supporters not to sit out the election. But Tories produced more of it in quantity than Whigs did. Neither side argued rationally (not even Defoe, for Harley, did that fully); Whigs played on fears of Jacobitism and renewed royal tyranny and religious intolerance. Still Whigs did try to argue that their experience in administration and finance went a long way toward insuring governmental effectiveness, especially in conducting a major war, and that the war was necessary and its prolongation was necessary until the French lost the possibility and had given up the hope of dominating Europe. Playing on fear was implicit in these two themes but more prominent was an intellectual emphasis on long-range policies and the importance of expertise in government. Whig writers probably won little additional support for such policies or for Whig views generally by such propaganda in the emotionalism of the election weeks. Nor was Whig traditional and emotional propaganda effective enough to offset Tory gains. If viscerally oriented propaganda bucked up nominal supporters on both sides Tories stood to gain because they had, as G. S. Holmes has said, a "natural majority of supporters in the political nation."[58]

58. *British Politics*, p. 248, and chap. 8 generally.

If they turned out most of their potential vote, Whigs had no chance of winning. The Tory vote did turn out with the anticipated results.

So it was in Kent where a full Tory turnout for the county election swamped the Whigs whose own vote was considerable. In 1708 the Tory candidates Dering and Hart had polled only 3,282 votes between them; the opposition had had 6,382. In 1710 the totals ran the other way: Dering and Hart got 7,080 and the other two candidates 5,377. The clergy made a concerted effort for Dering and Hart.[59] And some Tory or Tories gave the county special attention in *True English Advice to the Kentish Freeholders* (1710), which besides declaiming traditionally for the church and against the Whigs also subtly ranged into xenophobia, implying that the republican Dutch were so influential in English affairs that electors had better choose M.P.'s who would guard against "new laws . . . [to] alter the Best and most Happy form of Government on Earth." Whig clergy in Kent, on the other hand, were not numerous enough to be politically significant in 1710. And, although Lord Orford seems to have tried to help the Whig candidates by a circular letter his efforts were the only attempt at propaganda.[60] A local observer put his finger on the reason for Tory strength and Whig weakness in Kent: "the proceedings against Dr. Sacheverell have convinced a great number of men that no good was intended to the Church."[61]

The Tory victory came mainly from issues and in the freer constituencies, a judgment which assumes that Tories holding

59. Speck, "The House of Commons, 1702–1714," pp. 382, 402–403.

60. Ransome, "The General Election of 1710," p. 113, citing the *Post Boy*, September 20, 1710, which printed the letter.

61. Speck, "The House of Commons, 1702–1714," pp. 402–403.

safer seats continued to hold them after the elections were over. That they did, winning thirty-five new ones as well.[62] Even there issues became a test in 1710, more than occasionally superseding any hard personal political interests. In Wiltshire, noted for controlled elections since the Middle Ages, the Duke of Somerset was usually successful in having his way at Great Bedwyn and Marlborough, although the Bruce family contested his control. In 1705 Somerset's nominees had won both seats at Marlborough against the opposition of the Bruces and churchmen. In 1710 only one thing stood in the way of a reversal of this trend, according to Lord Bruce's agent in Marlborough, and that was Bruce's stand on Sacheverell: "If his Lordship, instead of being against was for the Doctor I am persuaded that nothing can hurt his interest."[63] Although Bruce had not voted on the impeachment, rumor had it that he was against Sacheverell. His agent thought that he should kill the story by giving Sacheverell money as others were doing. The gesture worked. Bruce's candidates won both seats at Marlborough and one at Bedwyn because he and they were for Sacheverell, while the Duke of Somerset "was against the Doctor."[64]

The Whig leader who suffered the greatest blow to his electoral interests was the Earl of Wharton.[65] Because of his position as lord lieutenant of Ireland, Wharton was absent during the crucial summer months when he needed to be tending

---

62. Derived by subtracting the number of new freer seats from Speck's totals for 1710.

63. H.M.C., Ailesbury MSS, pp. 201–202.

64. Ibid., See also *The Victoria History of the County of Wiltshire* (1957), v, 212–213.

65. The paragraph on Wharton draws heavily on the study of Wharton's connection by Walcott, *English Politics*, pp. 40, 200–202, and *Members of Parliament*.

his extensive interest which encompassed such far-flung areas as Buckinghamshire, Wiltshire, Westmorland, and Yorkshire. In the past Wharton had been well served for his efforts; his parliamentary interest rarely failed him. But 1710 undid the work of years.

In Yorkshire Sir William Hustler, a follower of Wharton who had been firmly entrenched in Northallerton, failed to win a seat there in 1710. In 1708 Wharton's interest had controlled at least seven seats in Buckinghamshire; but in 1710 this number was reduced to four, and one of these seats was held by Sir Richard Temple, a notoriously independent country squire. Both Wharton and his nominee, James Chase, had electoral interests in Marlow. Chase had served as a member for that borough since the beginning of the reign, but Marlow returned someone else in 1710. Richard Hampden, closely allied to Wharton, had a strong family interest at Wendover. Hampden not only lost the county election, which he had won in 1708, but was unable to secure even a seat at Wendover despite his interest there.[66] One of the cruelest blows to Wharton, however, must have been the election at Aylesbury of Sir Simon Harcourt, who had argued in Sacheverell's defense at the impeachment proceedings. Wharton had a special relationship with Aylesbury, whose burgesses in 1703 had come to pay him what they thought were last respects when he became seriously ill.[67] But the emotions of 1710 were strong enough to break even special relationships.

They were also strong enough to scare Whigs, watching

66. The Buckingham county election was one in which propaganda was used by the Tories on behalf of Lord Fermanagh. The *Supplement* for October 2 appealed for votes with a statement quite similar to the one used for the London election.

67. John Carswell, *The Old Cause: Three Biographical Studies in Whiggism* (1954), p. 97.

Tories sweep election after election, about their fate under a Tory ministry and Tory-dominated House of Commons. "God deliver us from such men and such principles,"[68] one of them wrote, forgetting in his despair that another general election would occur within three years and could alter party fortunes.

68. Holmes, *British Politics*, p. 409.

The General Election of 1713

V The election of 1710 had turned primarily on ideology, and Tories had won because they were right on the issues. They were right on the most important issue of 1713—peace—and won again, but their victory rested less on the strength of issues and more on the operation of electoral interests (governmental, private, and clerical) than it had in 1710. Tories had won so many seats in the counties and larger boroughs in 1710 that they could hardly make the same percentage of gains there in 1713. But the issue of trade, which divided Tories ideologically and on which the ministry misread the public, probably helped account for the nature of the Tory electoral victory. If peace itself had not been so popular Tories might not have done as well as they did. When the general election occurred the politically conscious were still euphoric enough to send thirty-two more Tories to Westminster than had been in the 1710 Parliament.

Soon after taking office in 1710 the new Tory ministry, while publicly professing no change of policy, secretly began negotiating with the French to end the war. English agents, but principally Henry St. John, worked out with the French Preliminary Articles of Peace which both countries signed in October, 1711. It still remained to be seen what the allies and the Whigs would say when they learned of the settlement. The Dutch were particularly incensed because few of the terms they expected from earlier English commitments in the Barrier Treaty of 1709 were in the articles. The Elector of Hanover accused the ministry of betraying the allied cause by leaving Spain in

Bourbon hands, and the Whigs moved in Parliament to force the ministry to renegotiate the articles so that they included the removal of the Bourbons from Spain.[1]

The ministry stopped the Whig maneuver and mounted propaganda campaigns against the Duke of Marlborough and the allies to rally support for its peace policies.[2] After being dismissed on charges of taking illicit commissions and blackened as an avaricious would-be dictator by Tory writers (chief among them Jonathan Swift, who had entered Harley's service in November, 1710[3]), Marlborough went into exile. Swift in *Conduct of the Allies* keynoted the campaign to convince the public that the allies had used England with Whig connivance, arguing that "no Nation was ever so long or so scandalously abused by the Folly, the Temerity, the Corruption, and the Ambition of its domestick Enemies; or treated with so much Insolence and Ingratitude by its foreign Friends" as England was. Numerous other pamphlets inspired by the ministry took up the theme, and the *Examiner* began in December, 1711, to expound on it. Evidence of broad support for moving against the allies followed the propaganda campaign (the *Conduct of the Allies* sold eleven thousand copies during the first month[4]), and the government did move in 1712. When the allies refused to sign the Preliminary Articles, the ministry ordered the British contingent on the Continent to withdraw from the allied armies. After the French had defeated the forces left in the allied com-

1. G. M. Trevelyan, *England under Queen Anne*, III (1934). Chapters 6, 11, 12, and 13 cover the negotiations and the signing of the Peace of Utrecht.

2. See Coombs, *The Conduct of the Dutch*, chaps. 10 and 11 for background to this paragraph.

3. On Swift, Harley, and St. John see Cook, *Jonathan Swift*, passim, and Stevens, *Party Politics*, chaps. 3 and 5.

4. Beljame, *Men of Letters*, p. 309.

mand, the Dutch and Germans quickly agreed to the articles and to the formal peace treaty which was signed at Utrecht in March and April, 1713.

The long-awaited peace produced as much rejoicing in England as news of Marlborough's victories had years before. Bonfires lit the summer nights throughout the country.[5] The all-important commercial provisions to the peace, however, produced mixed reactions. St. John (created Viscount Bolingbroke in 1712) had thought to cut the ground from under the Whigs by securing favorable commercial advantages for the trading classes and thus bind them to the ministry. But Whig leaders charged in Parliament, which still had to approve the commercial clauses of the treaty, that the clauses would ruin domestic manufacturing and impoverish England because they gave France a favorable balance of trade.[6] Alarmed by these charges the trading community submitted numerous testimonies to the detrimental effect of French trade under the treaty.

Even Tories themselves began to have second thoughts during the second reading in Commons. Sir Thomas Hanmer, the epitome of Toryism, a Tacker in 1704 and outspoken for peace itself, defected. He was followed by almost eighty Tories to oppose the clauses which failed to get a third reading. Hanmer's defection provides an insight into Tory psychology. He considered the clauses harmful to the country's economic interests, but he also feared the political alignment with France which such a commercial arrangement promoted and the threat this posed to the Protestant succession. Had Bolingbroke had his

5. Great Britain, Historical Manuscripts Commission, Report on the MSS of the Corporation of Chester, p. 395, Peter Shakerley to Mayor of Chester, April 4, 1713. Cited in later notes as H.M.C., Chester MSS.

6. See D. A. E. Harkness, "The Opposition to the 8th and 9th Articles of the Commercial Treaty of Utrecht," pp. 219–226.

way Hanmer and the "Hanoverian Tories," as they were dubbed, would have been driven from the party. Oxford (Harley had received an earldom in 1711) demurred, wanting to keep Tories from fragmenting.[7] That division could have happened as early as the election of 1713 instead of during the next year, because there was propaganda during the election which articulated a distinct Hanoverian Tory position on issues.[8]

The French commercial treaty was rejected in June, 1713, and the general election began in August, 1713—in those two months the ferment over peace, trade, and the succession continued. Partisan literature played a large part in keeping up public interest in issues. As usual the bulk of this propaganda was in the form of pamphlets or broadsides, many of which merely echoed the views put forward during the parliamentary debates on the treaty or were simply reprints of pieces written during the debates. Undoubtedly, too, much of the literature written in the spring was still circulating in the fall. Since 1710 several new journals had appeared. Others had ceased publication. The *Observator* ended in 1712; the *Medley* combined with the *Flying Post*; the *Review* ended in June, 1713. Oxford had given Defoe the job of defending the ministry's trade policies and he had begun the *Mercator* in May, 1713, for that purpose.[9] Whigs, principally Junto lords, started the *British Merchant* to oppose the *Mercator*. They also subvented, and

7. See Trevelyan, *England under Queen Anne*, III, 257–258, on the Tory defections.

8. *Instructions to the Freeholders Drawn from Her Majesty's . . . Speech* [July 17, 1713] *to Both Houses of Parliament* (1713) attacked Marlborough and defended the peace, but on the issue of trade it was aligned with the Whigs and urged voters to choose men who knew trade. The *Examiner* refused to castigate Hanmer and the defectors: no. 22, July 27–31, 1713.

9. See Stevens, pp. 52, 64–65, on the *Mercator*.

perhaps guided, Richard Steele's *Englishman* which appeared in the autumn of 1713 with the avowed purpose of opposing the ministry's *Examiner*.[10]

Whig propaganda on the issues of peace and trade meets many of the tests of an authentic party position. It was internally consistent, whether in the pieces anonymously penned or those clearly and directly inspired by Junto Whigs and Robert Walpole (who, incidentally, joined after 1710 to provide most of the Whig leadership until the end of the reign).[11] It drew upon and reaffirmed what had been since 1700 Whig views on foreign affairs and employed familiar devices of argumentation. It urged the election of men who subscribed to the Whig position. The charge that Tories had made a peace which left French power undiminished and which therefore wasted English lives and treasure issued out of traditional Whig foreign policy. Since 1700 Whigs had believed—pursuant to a balance of power theory—that the Bourbons had to be made to give up the Spanish throne if Europe was to see lasting peace. New to Whiggism was the charge that Tories had also attempted to betray the country to France by ruining the economy—although Whigs had long said Tories were French lackeys. For the more emotional who did indeed want to see "Bob and Harry [Oxford and Bolingbroke] hang'd" for the treaty, there was a squib which ran:

10. See Hanson, *Government and the Press*, pp. 101, 105, and Goldgar, *The Curse of Party*, pp. 125–126. For Steele's relations with the Junto see Goldgar, pp. 41, 53–54, 76–77, 99.

11. Holmes, *British Politics*, pp. 234–235. Joseph Addison, loyal Junto supporter, from 1712 until the end of the reign had a group of writers who met with him at Button's Coffeehouse in London: Stevens, pp. 17ff., and Goldgar, p. 30. See Stevens, pp. 28–29, for Walpole's use of writers and printers in 1713.

Oh! the wretched peace-makers,
Bob, Harry, Arthur, Matt
Who've lost our trade,
Our friends betray'd,
And all to serve a chamber-maid.
Oh! the wretched damn'd sham peace
That must our rents and stock decrease,
Must starve our poor,
And open the door
To let in a Popish Son of a Wh——.[12]

For the more thoughtful there were accounts of the effect the peace would have on the stability of Europe. Typically, one imagined England "a province of France" and Englishmen "so wretched that even slavery will be the least part of our misery."[13]

But the most famous Whig indictment of the peace and its makers was a pamphlet written by Robert Walpole after his imprisonment and exclusion from Commons in 1712 by the ministry for his leadership against the peace preliminaries.[14] *A Short History of the Parliament* recounted the history of the Parliament of 1710 which was dominated by Tories and laid heavy stress on its part in the making of peace. In marked contrast to Whig policy, Walpole said, was the new one Tories began: "the war must be ended, the Grand Alliance Dissolv'd, and to perfect all, Peace and a strict Friendship with France must

12. *A Satyr on the Earl of Oxford, Lord Bolingbroke, Mr. Moor and Mr. Prior.* The chambermaid was Abigail Hill who in 1710 had superseded the Duchess of Marlborough in the queen's affections. She was also a confidante of Oxford.

13. *Europe a Slave, When the Empire is in Chains* (1713). See also *Les Soupirs de L'Europe, etc., Or, the Groans of Europe at the Prospect of the Present Posture of Affairs* (1713).

14. See Plumb, *Walpole*, pp. 172–188.

be concluded." Tories trumped up charges of maladministration and corruption against the old ministry and decried the expense of the war. At the same time they levied heavier taxes than ever before and wasted the money. They agreed to the dishonorable peace with France and would have given away English commercial interests as well except that the "honest gentlemen" in Parliament rallied and threw out the bill of commerce. Voters would surely not want to "choose those again, who for the Characters of Loyal and Dutiful have sacrific'd their Country to the Power of France; which can end in nothing but bringing in the Pretender, Popery, and Slavery."

The peace was already signed, however, and Whig leaders probably knew there was little to be done about it. Trade, on the other hand, was an issue which might be exploited because of the opposition to the commercial clauses and the Jacobite tendency of the Tories which the clauses could be used to show. This propaganda did not have a wide popular appeal because of its liberal use of statistics and schemes of trade balances, but many merchants, tradesmen, and country gentlemen could understand the basic ideas, and they were the readers and voters for whom it was written. The issue, stated the first number of the *British Merchant*, was "whether France, after all her ill Successes in the late War, shall be suffer'd, during the present Peace, under the Colour of a Commerce, to exhaust our Treasure, beggar our Gentlemen, and starve our Common people? And whether the Gentlemen of Britain, after all their glorious Victories, will at last be contented to become Hewers of Wood, and Drawers of Water, to the Nation they have so often beaten?"[15] The basic argument of this journal and other pamphlets was that, since England produced little the French

15. *British Merchant,* I, no. I, August 7, 1713.

needed, when an exchange began England would wind up paying tremendous sums in bullion for French goods.[16] Not only that but the French trade would impair a profitable trade with Portugal, to which English merchants had been shipping large quantities of cloth in return for wine and gold. Said one writer, " 'Tis the Portugal Trade which has supported us in the War, and without it, we should soon find the Peace more burthensome than the War . . . The Trade with Portugal will Maintain, nay, Enrich our Poor; that with France, as stated in the Eighth and Ninth Articles, will Beggar and Undoe our Gentry."[17] The matter was not closed; a new Parliament could reopen the question, and therefore voters had to "prevent those Persons from being Chosen, who have already given their Votes for the 8th and 9th Articles,"[18] and choose, instead, men who voted against the bill, "Britons, and true Lovers of their Country."[19]

Tories also produced a great amount of propaganda on the issues of peace and trade. The ministry had lost the commercial clauses, but the peace itself was an issue on which all Tories agreed as did the public generally. In many senses there was also a Tory "press" on the issue of peace. Tories had opposed the war from the beginning; as early as the 1702 election they had said that the reason for the war was Whig greed for war profits. In 1710 they came out against the allies and for peace. Swift got

16. *Remarks on a Scandalous Libel Entitl'd: "A Letter From a Member of Parliament"* (1713). Other pamphlets were *Letter to a West Country Clothier and Freeholder* (1713) which Walpole either wrote or had someone write (Stevens, pp. 28–29); *The Trade With France, Italy, Spain, and Portugal, Considered* (1713); *A Letter to Sir R—— H——* (1713) and *General Maxims of Trade* (1713).

17. *Letter to a West Country Clothier.*

18. Ibid.

19. *Some Cautions Offered to the Consideration of those who Chuse Members to Serve in Parliament.*

suggestions on how to write; perhaps the *Examiner*'s authors did too, since Bolingbroke still managed the journal for the government.[20] Coordination of ideas may also have come from the Brother's Club which Bolingbroke began in 1711 and which included both politicians, Oxford, Bolingbroke, the Dukes of Ormonde, Beaufort, Sir William Wyndham, and George Granville among others, and writers such as Swift, Matthew Prior, John Arbuthnot, and John Freind. Coordination was what Bolingbroke had in mind for the group: "a number of valuable people will be kept in the same mind, and others will be made converts to their opinions.... The folly of our party will be ridiculed and checked; the opposition of another will be better resisted."[21]

Consistency and unity distinguished Tory writings on peace in the 1713 election: Whigs had stretched out the war for riches and power and had let the allies, mainly the Dutch, dupe England. One poem, *A Short Account of the Expiring Parliament,* took a swipe at the old Godolphin ministry and praised the Tory Parliament which

> Examin'd why, after great Battels won,
> The Conqueror was always most undone?
> Where the vast Sums of Treasure were convey'd
> Were by the injur'd People yearly paid?
> Why the poor Soldiers were so shortly fed
> When England paid so many Pounds for Bread?

A pamphlet written specifically against Robert Walpole, whom the ministry wanted to keep out of Commons because of his

---

20. See Cook, *Jonathan Swift*, p. xxix, and Stevens, chap. 3.

21. Gilbert Parke, ed., *Letters and Correspondence of Henry St. John, Viscount Bolingbroke* (1798), I, 246–247.

strong stand against peace, said Walpole and his fellow Whigs tried "to obstruct and delay the Blessing of Peace" because they relished "War, Blood, and Confusion, as their Oliverian Progenitors formerly did," and "preferr'd the Interest of an exotick State to that of their Native Kingdom."[22]

The *Examiner*[23] reflected the ministry's concern that the peace not be regarded as hastily contrived but "a safe, honourable, and in all human Probability, a lasting Peace" which gave the allies everything "which was in Justice due to them, or necessary to the common Safety and Repose of Europe." But Tories had at the same time "dissolv'd that fatal Confederacy, which pinn'd us down to other Nations, weaker than our own" and "sav'd our Treasure from being Drein'd to make Fat a strange Land, and enable the Inhabitants to Lord it over their Deliverers." The paper thought voters would want a new Parliament of "the Same Men again, I mean the Same in Temper, Principle, and Disposition."

Arguing for the trade policy of the ministry had been Defoe's job in the spring of 1713, and he continued to do so during the election. His task was not easy because he had to argue for a policy already defeated in Parliament and clearly unpopular, trade with the erstwhile enemy, refute an array of figures Whigs had adduced to show that England would lose by the French trade, and also justify a scheme whose full purpose he may not have known. Defoe's justifications were not necessarily ministerial intentions in making the commercial arrangements with France. Defoe did not deal with Bolingbroke, who had

---

22. *Cameronian Whigs no Patriots: Or, Some Remarkable Exploits of Bob Hush, and his Fairylanders, Set in a True Light in a Letter to an Elector of Lynn Regis.*

23. *Examiner*, IV, no. 23, July 31–August 3, 1713; no. 31, August 31–September 4, 1713. See also no. 29, August 24–28, 1713.

negotiated the clauses; he always worked for Oxford and, even though the latter had permitted the decision to seek a commercial treaty, Defoe had to understand the treaty through Oxford, not through its negotiator.

Defoe did believe the French trade was in England's interests and did not think the English economy would suffer. Some domestic interests would suffer, but such losses to France would be far outweighed by the wealth promised by the African and American trade under the treaty. Defoe believed in the soundness of the principle of free trade; he had so expressed himself in the *Review*, but not for electoral purposes. "Trade calculated for the General Good," he explained in the *General History of Trade* in July, "ought, as far as possible . . . to be extended and improved to the utmost, as the Universal Advantage of Nations." If men could "leave the World at rest, to pursue the just Advantages of Trade, every part of Europe would in a few Years be enrich'd by the General Circulation."[24] He did make a concession for electoral purposes to the balance-of-trade theory Whigs had employed by drawing up tables in the *General History* for September to show that the French would not enjoy special customs preferences under the commercial clauses. And in the *Memoirs of Count Tariff* he made even greater concessions to electoral purposes by charging that the Whig outcries over the trade issue were instigated by the Dutch who wanted the trade with France all to themselves and had had Whigs excite and misinform people so that the bill of commerce would be rejected.[25] The effects of Defoe's

24. On the *General History of Trade* see W. H. Bonner, "Moll, Knapton, and Defoe: A Note on Early Serial Publication," pp. 322–323.

25. The *Examiner*, IV, no. 32, September 4–11, 1713, also made this charge, which argues for ministerial coordination of its propaganda on this issue.

propaganda efforts we will examine in election contests themselves.

Even more difficult for the ministry and Tories to argue than the issue of trade was the issue of the succession. The queen was obviously not going to live much longer, and the Act of Settlement designating the Protestant succession had not really settled the matter.[26] The large contingent of Jacobites in Commons after 1710; ideology, which caused many other Tories to be tugged between the Pretender and the Hanoverian line; the making of the Treaty of Utrecht which had angered the Elector of Hanover; and the ministry's entanglement in schemes to restore the Pretender on Anne's death—all these things made the succession a very difficult issue psychologically for Tories and the ministry. Whigs sensed this and Whig leaders knew of the Jacobite schemes, probably because they too were in communication with the Pretender's court.[27] Whigs always seemed to feel that they had an advantage on issues related to the revolution settlement. In 1713 they had an additional motive for pushing the succession issue: under increased psychological pressure Hanoverian Tories might again bolt from the ministry and other Tories. That was the Whig aim, as even Tories understood: "they give up the distinction of Whig and Tory, and bend all their thoughts to make new distinction between the Tories themselves, as Hanover Tory and Pretender Tory, English Tory and French Tory, for trade and against it."[28]

Most of what Whigs wrote was, indeed, about the immediate question of the succession instead of the more general topics

---

26. See *Englishman*, I, no. 5, October 15, 1713, for a comment about the daily discussion of the succession about town. I have used Rae Blanchard's fine edition, *The Englishman: A Political Journal* (1955).

27. See Trevelyan, *England under Queen Anne*, III, chap. 16.

28. H.M.C., Dartmouth MSS, p. 319, Erasmus Lewis to Oxford, October 1, 1713.

of hereditary right, resistance, passive obedience, and divine right monarchy which they usually discussed at length in election literature.[29] Robert Walpole had a hand in this propaganda, perhaps a major managerial hand in an enterprise which seems to have involved not only "the Best Pens" but those "employ'd in the private Printing and Dispersing of several Papers . . . against the Enemies of the Protestant Succession."[30] Two of the works were the *Letter to the West Country Clothier* and Walpole's own *Short History of the Parliament*, both of which asserted that a ministerial scheme of restoring the Pretender lay behind the commercial clauses of the peace treaty. Richard Steele, long a supporter of Wharton, Somers, and Halifax of the Junto, joined these efforts in the *Englishman*. Steele took the view that all the talk about the Pretender's right to the throne was mere caviling. The Protestant succession was law; the Act of Settlement had fixed the line of succession and no question of hereditary right could alter it. The Pretender was even "a Traytor to this nation; and we all remember him the Invader of it. . . . By all Laws Divine and Humane he is an utter Stranger to us."[31] The anonymous writer of *Letter to the Gentlemen and Freeholders of the County of Dorset* thought the Hanoverian succession ought to be made the test for candidates. He urged electors to inquire "Whether the Persons who they design shall represent them . . . are true Friends to the Hanover Succession." Members of Parliament "ought to be such as dare not look to, or so much as think on, the Pretender or have the least Hopes of his coming amongst us; no! they

29. However *The Judgment of Whole Kingdoms and Nations* (1713), a treatise against passive obedience and hereditary right was circulated during elections in 1713.

30. Stevens, p. 29. And then there was Addison's group at Button's referred to in note 11 above.

31. *Englishman*, I, no. 5, October 15, 1713.

ought to be such, as will with all their utmost Force, Interest and Power oppose and resist him, when ever he, or Popery (which is the same thing) shall meditate a Return into these Nations."[32]

Understandably the ministry had little to say about the succession. The *Examiner* did reply feebly to the Whig charges by recalling that Tories had removed "the Pretender further off, and convinced the World (if the other Party are Sincere) that we all agree in the Protestant Succession, as our Common Interest and Security." The paper was also sure that "preserving the Prerogative and Honour of the Crown and of unloading it from Debts at home, and foreign Dependence, which recommended us to the Favour of the Person in Possession, would be equally successful in procuring us the perfect Friendship of a wise and discerning Successor."[33] But there were no lengthy defenses of passive obedience or hereditary right in the ministry's propaganda.

Jacobite propaganda did appear during the elections, which might imply that what the ministry did not want to do publicly in the *Examiner* it tried to do clandestinely, namely inspire Jacobite hopes as a contingency against the Pretender's restoration. That would presuppose that the ministry was unified in its thinking on the succession when all indications are to the contrary. By 1713 Bolingbroke was working toward leadership of the Jacobite wing of the party and did succeed in forming such a faction in the 1713 Parliament. In doing that he broke

---

32. However, since this pamphlet questioned the passage of the Occasional Conformity Bill of 1711, which the Junto had helped pass, it may have come instead from an independent Whig.

33. *Examiner,* IV, no. 23, July 31—August 3, 1713. Ironically the motion to address the queen to see about having the Pretender removed from countries friendly to Britain after he had to leave France was a Whig motion and the ministry was reluctant to implement it (Holmes, *British Politics*, p. 85).

with Oxford, who entertained Jacobite schemes but never committed himself to them.[34] It is consonant with Bolingbroke's activities for a Jacobite bloc that he should have at least taken part in the instigation of Jacobite propaganda. His interest in propaganda dissemination and his managerial experience in it also give us reasons, even if slight ones, to argue as we do.

Bolingbroke knew those who were actually doing the writing very well. One of his associates from the early period of the *Examiner* and a member of his faction in the Parliament of 1713, Francis Atterbury, produced some of the High Tory propaganda. With Henry Sacheverell, Atterbury delivered sermons on High Tory principles, which tended to promote the Pretender's restoration, and printed the sermons for wider distribution.[35] Some Jacobites tacked up the title page from one High Tory tract, *The Hereditary Right of the Crown of England Asserted*, on church doors and in prominent places.[36] High Tory adaptations of the Psalms were circulated as *The Loyal Man's Psalter*. And Jacobites sent anonymous letters to mayors and magistrates around the country, urging that they come out for the Pretender and implying that the queen and ministry would approve. The election of between eighty and a hundred Jacobites to the new Parliament indicates there were receptive listeners for such propaganda.[37] It at least offered a definite policy for Tories which the *Examiner* failed to do.

---

34. Holmes, *British Politics*, pp. 270, 279–280.

35. See William H. Lecky, *A History of England in the Eighteenth Century* (1879), I, 158–160, for the Jacobite propaganda discussed in this paragraph.

36. Walpole later charged and offered to show proof that the pamphlet itself had been researched in the state files at public expense. Was this done by Bolingbroke, instead of Oxford, to whom Walpole attributed it? (Stevens, pp. 27–28).

37. See Holmes, *British Politics*, pp. 279–280, for the Jacobites in Commons.

If the ministry did not and could not stir itself on the succession, it did have something to say about the church and toleration. This was not a major issue in 1713 compared to the issues of peace and trade, but the Sacheverell affair of 1710 had not been forgotten. An Occasional Conformity Bill had been passed in 1711, even if a watered-down one because Whigs had traded a mild bill's passage for the Earl of Nottingham's assistance for the "No Peace Without Spain" motion.[38] Many Tories had long wanted a stiffer bill than that of 1711. Dissenters were so fearful that they would enact one that they had generally voted with Whigs. Oxford had sought and won Dissenter support before (for example, from the Quaker William Penn in 1708[39]), and perhaps he thought that the Junto's action had made some Dissenters willing to consider supporting the government (which would help offset High Tory pressure on him). The effort to win Dissenters was not a large one, and it was a mixture of reason and threat. The *Examiner*[40] urged Dissenters to "leave the tents of these Wicked Whigs," since Whigs had passed the Occasional Conformity Bill. They would have given up the toleration too, the paper said, to serve their own interests. But Dissenters could rely on the queen's goodness to keep laws against them in suspension providing that they did not take the Whigs' side against the government. Defoe in *A Letter to the Dissenters* said the same things. Why should Dissenters "embroil themselves with the Government . . . and hazard all their Religious Advantages, which now they enjoy, in the private Quarrel of a Faction?" That would only "oblige the Government to teach them their own Interest by

38. Ibid., p. 113.

39. See H.M.C., Portland MSS, IV, 461.

40. *Examiner*, IV, no. 28, August 21–24, 1713. Also no. 23, July 31–August 3, 1713.

Methods more mortifying than they otherwise intended to do." He meant that the government would allow the penalties of the Occasional Conformity Bill to fall on the Dissenters with full force.

Whigs, especially the Junto Whigs, were understandably reluctant to delve into the last three years because of their role in passing the Occasional Conformity Bill. So Whig propaganda on the issue of the church was limited to stock arguments about moderation, toleration, and attacks on High Churchmen. *Remarks on a Scandalous Libel*[41] advised the "Honest British Freeholder to chuse Men that are Loyal to Her Majesty and zealous for the Church . . . That are for Toleration to Dissenters, and doing no more to make em Jealous and Uneasy . . . That do not Cry out the Church, and mean that of Rome." And another pamphlet wanted voters to "enquire whether the candidates are Men moderate in their Principles."[42]

Trade, of all the issues surveyed above, seemed to be of greatest moment in the counties and more democratic boroughs. In both Wiltshire and Buckinghamshire partisan differences on trade with France caused very turbulent elections. Whigs in both contests, as elsewhere in the country, made wool their party symbol, saying graphically what Whig propaganda had said: English domestic industries (chief of which was the woollen industry) would be destroyed by French trade. In Wiltshire "the Whig party appeared (all of them) with wool in their hats at the place of election. The Tories hooted them, called them wolves in sheep's clothing, surrounded them by parcels and whipped many of them and knocked down others, insomuch that the Whigs were soon forced to pull all the wool out

41. Which echoed the Junto's views on trade and peace and probably was Junto-inspired.

42. *Letter to the Gentlemen and Freeholders of the County of Dorset.*

of their hats." Whigs charged bribery, intimidation by a Tory-hired mob, and unfairness by the returning officer who kept Quakers from voting for the Whig candidates they had intended to vote for (Quaker voting intentions suggest that Oxford's campaign to woo Dissenters to his side did not have a broad appeal). The Tories won by nearly six hundred votes.[43] They also won in Buckinghamshire where the Earl of Wharton himself led Whigs to the polling place wearing wool in his hat. His wife "with her own fair hands" made woolen cockades and handed them out to the crowd. Tories, however, shouted that the Whigs "looked very sheepish, and ba'd them out of the field."[44]

In the Sussex county election[45] Henry Campion, a proponent of the bill of commerce and a strong Jacobite, won a seat despite stiff opposition including a written appeal in the *Flying Post* to voters not to support him because he had "voted for the Bill of Commerce with France which was rejected by the late Parliament." His opponents were "men zealously affected to the present constitution both in Church and State, the Queen, and Protestant Succession in the Illustrious House of Hanover, and for the encouragement of the Woolen manufacture." Campion seems not to have had propaganda written specifically for his support, although London—and propaganda published there for the Tory side—was not very far away. The *Mercator* especially was being sent out to such constituencies "that they may make choice of better Friends to this Bill for the next Par-

---

43. For the Wiltshire county election see the *Victoria History of Wiltshire*, v, 199, and H.M.C., Ailesbury MSS, p. 212.

44. For the Buckingham county election see Carswell, *The Old Cause*, pp. 120–121, and Verney, ed., *The Verney Letters*, I, 314–315.

45. For Sussex see the *Flying Post* for August 22–25, 1713.

liament. For this end the *Mercator* travels every Week throughout the Country . . . his readers have him *gratis*."[46]

Trade was also the chief issue in London which, through the testimonies of its merchants in Parliament against the bill of commerce, had already indicated its opposition to the ministry's trade policy. Three of the incumbent Tories had voted against the commercial treaty, which probably gave Whigs hope that London might choose Whig opponents of the bill as well as Tory opponents. Whigs set up "Four eminent merchants"[47] who disapproved of the treaty and wrote propaganda specifically for the election. Some of it flattered city merchants: "The Merchants are like so many Centinels placed in all the Nations of the World to watch over and defend her. And will not this City chuse such as these for her Representatives? Will she who subsists wholly by Trade, rather chuse such who are unacquainted with it even in Theory?"[48] *Advice to the Liverymen of London* warned that "Trade never perhaps needed more than now to have Skilful and Vigilant Guardians" and hoped that "there is no Citizen of London to be taught now what to think of such as Voted for that Bill then, or repent of their Voting against it." The incumbents had commercial connections and three of them had opposed the bill, so that, while Whig propaganda might have cut into their lead, it could hardly have persuaded electors to throw out men who had the qualifications it said M.P.'s ought to have. In fact it seems to have helped Tories as much as Whigs, since all four Tories

46. *British Merchant*, I, no. 1, August 7, 1713. If the *Mercator* helped Campion, it did not do all the ministry had hoped, as the results below indicate.

47. F. Elrington Ball, ed., *The Correspondence of Jonathan Swift* (1911), II, 77–80, Swift to Archbishop King, October 20, 1713.

48. *Englishman*, no. 3, October 10, 1713.

won in a close poll. A Tory victory under those circumstances tends to confirm the unpopularity of the bill of commerce without vindicating the Whigs' stand on other issues.

Not only Tories against the ministry's trade policy were returned by the more democratic constituencies, but Whigs were also. Robert Walpole's election was one Tories tried the hardest to prevent because of his opposition in the preceding Parliament and his writings against the Treaty of Utrecht and the proposed trade with France.[49] Tories indicated how important his defeat was by publishing several pamphlets attacking him by name. An especially scurrilous piece entitled *The Testimonies of Several Citizens of Fickleborough in the Kingdom of Fairyland Concerning the Life and Character of Robert Hush, Commonly Called Bob* said his ancestors were republicans with "the greatest Inclination to the Government, which was the most Imperfect and Deformed," and charged that "he had been caballing at Taverns, Horse-Races, and such like places how to depose the Queen," that he was in the French interest and that he had purposely obstructed the peace settlement. It also said that he was a "Lewd, Dissolute, and Profane Person" who in his younger days had "persuaded his sister to be an whore in order to get preferment." *Cameronian Whigs No Patriots*, already cited earlier in the chapter, attacked him as a war profiteer who preferred Dutch interests to his own country's.

Whig propaganda would seem not to have been produced in Walpole's behalf, if we go by the lack of reference to pamphlets or papers which called specifically for his election. That seems odd since Walpole himself had had a hand in the writing

49. The following paragraphs have drawn heavily from Plumb, *Walpole*, pp. 172–188.

and distribution of propaganda for other elections. The victory speech he gave after his election, however, identified major Whig concerns in the election.[50] The last Tory Parliament had allowed the Pretender to wait in exile "as near as the power of France can place him." As for peace, he thought the French king, had he won, would "have given us better terms than we have gained after all our glorious victories." A third concern, toleration, he thought would be threatened again by the new Parliament which probably would be Tory controlled, but he promised to "struggle hard for our religion and liberty." The speech seems to take it for granted that electors knew something of the issues already and knew why the Whig position on these issues was the right one. The propaganda we surveyed earlier in the chapter could have given them such knowledge. So could letters Walpole probably sent from London or those from his Norfolk colleagues in Parliament who continued sitting after he was expelled and imprisoned, and who probably sent back accounts of the parliamentary proceedings with interpretations. Such information and interpretation were part of the shaping of opinion and preparation for partisan voting in parliamentary elections.

Most Whigs in 1713 were not so successful as Walpole had been. But election results in the counties and larger boroughs suggest that Whig agitation and propaganda against the commercial treaty with France had had unexpected consequences. Whigs themselves did not profit from their propaganda and opposition nearly as much as Tories who also opposed the bill. Fifty-seven percent of Whigs who opposed the bill were re-elected, indicating the importance of trade in winning contests in a general election in which Whigs otherwise were falling

50. H.M.C., Portland MSS, v, 333.

far behind Tories. Seventy-nine percent of the Tories who had voted against the bill were reelected, compared to 75 percent of the Tories who had supported the bill, which suggests that even electors who chose Tories had strong sympathies for the Whig position on trade if not for Whiggism itself. The results from all the constituencies do not produce a pattern quite so clear. Overall reelected supporters of the bill barely outnumbered opponents (132 to 131).[51] But the ministry had ample reason, if it needed or wanted it, not to push the measure again since so many of the bill's opponents would be back in Commons. When Parliament reconvened trade was not even mentioned. Even if a pattern of election results indicating a strong preference for the bill had emerged, the ministry probably would not have reopened the matter because Tories were divided on other issues, especially the succession, and Oxford's preference was to avoid divisive issues when possible. The election of a large number of Jacobites reflected no national uneasiness about the question of the succession, despite the fact that the Whig leaders and writers had worried about it and Tories had divided over it. Nor did the issue of peace seem to cause national division. The country accepted it gratefully and almost wholeheartedly with the exception of staunch Whigs.

The country also accepted the peacemakers, returning a Tory majority of better than two to one.[52] Unlike the experience of 1710, many of these new seats seem to have been gathered in the more narrowly based franchises by ministerial efforts and those of Tory leaders, by the clergy, and by newcomers. Oxford

---

51. The statistics come from checking those who voted on the bill (lists are appended to *Remarks on a Scandalous Libel*, a Whig pamphlet, and *A Letter from a Member of the House of Commons*, 1713, a Tory pamphlet) against *Members of Parliament*, pt. 2, pp. 29–36.

52. See Speck, "The House of Commons, 1702–1714," pp. 418ff.

was much more active in using governmental influence for electioneering than he had been in 1710. The reason was that he thought (erroneously but with some justification) that Tories were not likely to get the large majority in 1713 that they had had in 1710. He thought it necessary for the government to bestir itself to make sure of a working majority.[53] Among the things he could do was the changing of key local officials before contests began and the cultivation of the government's interest in the Scottish elections. He did both.[54] He also relied on allies such as George Granville, Lord Lansdowne, Tory "whip" for Cornwall and Devon. Discounting Lansdowne's well-known enthusiasm, it is still true that his efforts were prodigiously successful: "we compute ourselves to have a majority of ten to one to be depended upon . . . in which no less than twenty are of my own nomination."[55] Oxford also negotiated for and won part of the old Godolphin interest in Cornwall through Bishop Trelawney (Godolphin having died in 1712).[56] And in Wales where Oxford's own electoral interest was strongest Tories triumphed as completely as in 1710.[57]

Clergy also enlarged the Tory majority considerably as one of them reported in Kent: "this time 3 years [ago] there were ten Whigs elected in this county and but 8 Church-men: now we have 13 Church-men, and but 5 Whigs. I pray God that we may have equal success in other counties: and the truth is I think the settlement and future peace of the nation do entirely

53. Holmes, *British Politics*, p. 352.

54. H.M.C., Portland MSS, v, 345, The Earl of Findlater to Oxford, October 8, 1713.

55. Ibid., pp. 330–331, Lord Lansdowne to Oxford, September 11, 1713.

56. Ibid., p. 329, Jonathan, Bishop of Winchester to Oxford, September 11, 1713: "In obedience to your commands I have taken care to have Mr. Jenning's chosen at East Looe."

57. Ibid., pp. 326–327. Cf. also *Members of Parliament.*

depend upon a good majority of honest Church-men in the L[ower] House."[58] Many new Tories, too, came to Westminster as replacements for men unwilling to run again because of the expenses of the contests and of living in London several months each year. One estimate put the total number of newcomers at over two hundred.[59] Most of them were Tories. So far as the government was concerned they were an unstable element in Commons, similar to the group which had made up the October Club and had harassed the ministry since the last general election.

Tory victories were the losses of Whig interests such as those of the Earl of Wharton and the Russell family. In the months preceding the elections Wharton had been tireless in canvassing the various constituencies and attempting to repair his magnificent electoral machine.[60] During the Buckinghamshire elections he appeared personally to forward his interest at Marlow which had until 1710 usually elected his nominee and Sir James Etheredge, a Tory. In 1713 the borough again did not choose Wharton's nominee; it returned both incumbent Tories by an overwhelming majority. Wendover did elect two friends and Wycombe elected one, but these were only three seats, which meant two less than Wharton had won in 1710 in the county. Wharton's friends fared little better in Yorkshire elections. Five of them had won seats in 1710, three at boroughs Wharton influenced and two at the large freeman borough of Hull. In 1713 the number dropped to four. In Wiltshire, however, Wharton's interest suffered most. The election of 1710 in which only four of his friends had been elected had seemed disastrous but

58. Holmes and Speck, *The Divided Society*, p. 137.

59. See Holmes, *British Politics*, p. 180, for the estimate by the Hanoverian envoy.

60. See Carswell, pp. 120–121.

the election of 1713 was worse. Only one of his followers can be recognized among the election returns for the county—Joseph Addison, the Whig writer, elected for Malmesbury. Wharton's total following in the new Parliament is very difficult to assess, but it was obviously far below the number in the Parliament of 1710.[61] Perhaps the greatest upset among Whig leaders occurred in Bedfordshire where the Russells had long been entrenched behind territorial influence. Even the Tory triumph of 1710 had left their electoral interest undisturbed. But something went wrong in 1713. No Russell sat for the county seat usually held by Edward Lord Russell and at Bedford borough only one recognizable Russell follower was elected.[62]

In the light of the election results, Thomas Burnet's pre-election hope that Whigs could "take off the heads of these Bloody Peace-makers"[63] after they won the general election was utterly naive. Tories came back to Westminster in greater numbers than ever. But they came back with schisms which always weakened them more than Whig opposition could. In the remaining months of Anne's reign, while the Tory leaders, Oxford and Bolingbroke, quarreled and maneuvered, the mass of Tories were left with no clear course of action. When the queen's long-expected demise came in August, 1714, it sounded the death knell of what Sir Keith Feiling called the first Tory party.

---

61. Cf. *Members of Parliament*, pt. 2, pp. 29–36. I am using the study of Wharton's connection by Walcott, *English Politics*, pp. 39–41, 200–202, 229–232.

62. Cf. *Members of Parliament* and Walcott, *English Politics*, pp. 44, 176, 181.

63. Holmes, *British Politics*, pp. 114–115.

Conclusion

Bishop Burnet, writing before the end of Anne's reign, detested the necessity of using the labels "Whig" and "Tory." They were, he said, "terms that I have much spoken against, and even hated; but to avoid making always a longer description, I must use them, they being now become as common as if they had been words of our language."[1] Studies of election propaganda reaffirm Burnet's judgment that "Whig" and "Tory" were essential descriptions of party activity. The studies also leave little room for doubting that parties having broad principles, assumptions, and attitudes did exist. Their reality is attested to by the electoral continuity and durability of issues, of perspectives on issues and of techniques and devices for arguing them, and by appeals to voters to elect candidates on the basis of issues.

Whiggism, like Toryism, drew from and grew out of the Exclusion Crisis of 1679–1681 and the partisan struggles of William III's last years. It was animated by fear of French power and by the conviction that foreign interventionism was necessary to keep the revolution settlement safe at home. Whiggism was also driven by the assumption that Toryism was an internal menace because it welcomed the Pretender and the French, who would crush the revolution settlement and install absolutism. Exactly who instigated the "party" writing of 1702 is not clear; probably the Junto was responsible for much of it since it supported Junto policies and maneuvers of the pre-

1. *History of My Own Time*, IV, 6.

ceding half-dozen years. Whiggism was reshaped in 1705 at the Junto's instigation to bear on the tacking incident and to support the governmental call for moderation, but was still discernibly Whig. On the traditional issues—church, revolution, and war—Whig writings in 1708 were mainstream Whiggism. The Junto-inspired propaganda which attacked the government for corruption and mismanagement and defended Tories who had accepted the revolution settlement was an aberration from tradition. The reasons for that aberration no longer existed by the election of 1710. The Whig ideological position, instigated to a high degree by the Junto again, reflected intensified Whig concerns for the Continental land war to contain French aggression and for the revolution settlement, both of which were threatened by a resurgent Toryism. The war had been ended before the last general election of the reign but, according to Whiggism, not before the possibility of a French hegemony in Europe had been eliminated. Whigs charged that the French, supposedly the losers, had gotten better concessions than the victors because Tories schemed thereby to restore the Pretender, popery, and French absolutism on the queen's death. Especially vital to Whiggism of 1713 was opposition to the trade with France which the ministry had wanted and lost in a parliamentary vote. This propaganda was clearly commissioned and closely coordinated by the Junto and another Whig leader, Robert Walpole.

Toryism was less coherent as an ideology or party position because Tories had real problems of conscience over the revolution settlement and especially the succession. And yet Toryism was an authentic ideological position on the church, the revolution settlement, and the war. In 1702 it was compounded of fear of domestic subversion and of isolationism in foreign affairs. Tories were isolationists because they thought that irreligious republican Whigs within the state and church were more dangerous than the French without. Whiggism, to Tories, threatened the religious and constitutional foundations of society. The consequence of Whiggism was anarchy such as in 1641; the only bulwark against that was a purified Whigless church. Because the Tory position in 1702 also included attacks on the previous Junto-dominated ministry and its advocacy of the land war in Europe, it seems probable that the New Country coalition of Harley and High Tory leaders—Rochester, Nottingham, and Seymour—inspired much of this propaganda. By 1705 the coalition had been broken by Harley's alignment with the government against the High Tory leaders. The latter reaffirmed the traditional position on the church and defended their attempts to tack the Occasional Conformity Bill to the land tax as necessary to national safety and tranquility. High Tories also argued Toryism in 1708 doggedly defending passive obedience and divine-right monarchy as natural and divinely ordained, reiterating the church's being in danger, and hinting that the war would have been ended long before if Whigs had not wanted to line their pockets. By 1710 the war had become unpopular and the public was in a spoiling mood. People were ready to believe that the war was unnecessary, that Whigs had gotten rich off public money, and that the church was threatened, as Sacheverell said, by such false brethren. The instigation of much of that propaganda clearly came from the new Tory government; the rest came from private sources, surely some from the clergy, and perhaps some from High Tory leaders. In the election of 1713 Toryism was principally a justification of the recent peace and the proposed trade with France, the Tory ministry again inspiring most of the party writings. Forthright Jacobitism also appeared in election propaganda as part of the Tory position. Its origin is uncertain, but it undoubtedly came from one of the forming Jacobite factions. It may have been inspired by the one led by Bolingbroke.

In addition to the two positions which were within the mainstreams of Whiggism and Toryism, there was a third point of view prominent in 1705 and 1710 and not within either of the partisan traditions. This was the moderation and consensus campaign of Harley to draw support from both Whigs and Tories. Even that exception to Whig and Tory ideological positions was a "party" view with continuity of themes, techniques, and devices and with an appeal to electors that they choose men for Parliament on the basis of ideas and political behavior.

Given that "parties" as ideologies existed and were the bases for electoral appeals, what impact did these party positions and issues have? It is true that Tories would not have had majorities in the Parliaments of 1702 and 1713 if they had not been able to win large numbers of seats among the smaller constituencies. Whigs would not have commanded a majority in 1708 without similar victories. But there is much evidence to confirm the hypothesis that party in the ideological sense did make a difference in election results. Those constituencies to which ideology appealed because they were relatively free from political control (the counties, universities, and larger boroughs) did often reflect electoral trends much more sharply than other constituencies, suggesting the influence of issues and party views. The clearest instance of this was the Tory victory of 1710 which came mainly in the freer constituencies, but there is evidence that greater percentages of victories or defeats in those franchises, as the case might be from election to election, also occurred in the elections of 1702, 1705, and, perhaps, 1708. Individual contests throughout the period also seemed to turn on issues and propaganda.

Whiggism and Toryism were principles, attitudes, and assumptions which led to certain rather well-defined patterns of thought and action on the major issues of the period. These were the distinctions which most men of the age, but especially those in the county, university, and larger borough electorates, widely recognized and of which they generally approved. Judging from the ideological continuity we discovered, the vast majority of Englishmen would have been offended by the proclamation of interests or connections as the basis for party distinctions or for choosing M.P.'s (significant though these connections were in coordinating election efforts). There was something sinister and immoral about the idea of a tightly organized unit of members who operated as a phalanx in Parliament as a modern party does. The literature of the period was replete with diatribes against "cabals" and "factions" which pursued their own interests rather than the interests of the nation at large. There were parliamentary interests, but even the most cynical politicians did not dare openly proclaim the existence of these groups or campaign during the elections on mere factional interests. They had to garb their activities and designs in acceptable ideological dress to appeal to the sensitivities of the great number of gentry, burgesses, and clergy for whom it was true, as one pamphleteer said, that "the General Method of Enquiry about Members for Parliament is, whether they are Whigs or Tories."[2]

2. *A Letter to the Gentlemen and Freeholders of the County of Dorset* (1713).

Bibliography

I. Contemporary Works

A. Pamphlets

An Account of the Test Offer'd to the Consideration of the Electors of Great Britain. London, 1710.

Advice to All Freeholders and Other Electors for the Ensuing Parliament: Some Reflections upon the Foregoing Paper. [London, 1705.]

Advice to the Gentlemen Freeholders, and All Others That Have a Just Right To Send Representatives to Parliament in South Britain. N.p., 1710.

Advice to the Livery-Men of London: Showing That It is for Their Interest and Honour To Chuse Merchants in Trade for Their Representatives in Parliament with Seasonable Cautions to Them, on the Approaching Elections. London: Ann Baldwin, 1713.

Bodkins and Thimbles: or 1645 Against 1710. N.p., 1710.

[Boyer, Abel.] *Letter from a Foreign Minister in England to Monsieur Pettecum Minister of Holstein Containing the True Reasons of the Late Changes in the Ministry, and of the Calling a New Parliament: and Therefore Fit To Be Perus'd by All the Electors.* 1st ed. London: John Baker, 1710.

The Calamity of the Church of England Under a Presbyterian Government Made Visible. London, 1710.

The Cameronian Whigs No Patriots, or Some Remarkable Exploits of Bob Hush [Walpole] and His Fairylanders, Set in a True Light, In a Letter to an Elector of Lynn Regis. London: John Morphew, 1713.

The Candidates. London: John Baker, 1713.

The Case Fairly Stated, in a Dialogue Between Moderation and Constitution. London: Thomas Warren, 1702.

The Case of Moderation and Occasional Communion Represented by Way of Caution to the True Sons of the Church of England. 1st ed., 1704; reprinted London: Richard Wilkin, 1705.

Cautions to Those Who Chuse Members To Serve in Parliament, to Which Is Added a List of Those Who Voted for and Against the Bill of Commerce, as Published in "A Letter from a Member of the House of Commons to His Friend in the Country." London: John Baker, 1713.

The Character of a Sneaker. 2nd ed. London: Benjamin Bragg, 1705.

Character of a Tacker. London, 1705.

Considerations on Peace and War: 1, Whether it be the Interest of the Allies to Consent to a Lasting Peace in the Conjuncture; 2, upon what Conditions a Lasting Peace may be Expected; 3, the Means for Obtaining Such Conditions. London, 1710.

Considerations Relating to our Choice, and the Qualifications of our Members of Parliament. London, 1710.

The Countryman's Remembrancer to Sir H[umphr]y M[ackwor]th, Sir E[dwar]d S[eymou]r, Sir J[oh]n P[ackingto]n . . . and the Rest of the most Honourable Members who were most for Promoting the Bill Against Hypocracie, Heresie, and Schism alias Occasional Conformity . . . London, 1705.

[Davenant, Charles.] *Essays upon Peace at Home and War Abroad*. 2 pts. 2nd ed. London: John Knapton, 1704.

[———.] *Sir Thomas Double at Court and in High Preferments; in Two Dialogues Between Sir Tho. Double and Sir Rich. Comover, Alias Mr. Whiglove, on the 27 of Sept. 1710*. London: John Morphew, 1710.

[———.] *Tom Double Return'd out of the Country: or the True Picture of a Modern Whig Set Forth in a Second Dialogue Between Mr. Whiglove and Mr. Double*. 1st ed. London: John Nutt, 1702.

[———.] *The True Picture of an Ancient Tory: A Dialogue Between a Vassal, a Tory, and Freeman, a Whig.* London, 1702.

A Debate Between Three Ministers of State on the Present Affairs of England in Relation to the Disposition of the Nation at Home, our Alliances Abroad, and the Designs of France. London, 1702.

[Defoe, Daniel.] *Advice to All Parties.* 2nd ed. London: Benjamin Bragg, 1705.

[———.] *Essay upon Public Credit; Being an Enquiry how the Publick Credit Comes to Depend upon the Change of the Ministry, or the Dissolutions of Parliaments, and Whether it does or no; with an Argument Proving that Publick Credit may be Upheld and Maintained in this Nation, and Perhaps Brought to a Greater Height than it ever yet Arrived at.* London, 1710.

[———.] *General History of Trade.* 4 pts. London: John Baker, 1713.

[———.] *King William's Affection to the Church of England Examin'd.* 3rd ed. London, 1703.

[———.] *A Letter to the Dissenters.* 1st ed. London: John Morphew, 1713.

[———.] *Memoirs of Count Tariff, By Which the Whole Secret History of the Refusing the Late Treaty of Peace is Laid Open.* 1st ed. London: John Morphew, 1713.

[———.] *A New Test of the Sence of the Nation: Being a Modest Comparison Between the Addresses to the late King James, and those to her Present Majesty.* N.p., 1710.

[———.] *A Word Against a New Election, That the People May See the Happy Difference Between English Liberty and French Slavery and May Consider Well Before They Make the Exchange.* London, 1710.

A Dialogue Between Jack High and Will Low: Proper for the Perusal of Those Who Have a Right to Choose for the Ensuing Parliament. London, 1710.

A Dialogue Betwixt Whig and Tory, Alias Williamite and Jacobite. Wherein . . . the Principles and Practices of Each Party Are

Fairly and Impartially Stated; that Thereby Mistakes and Prejudices May be Removed.... 1693; reprinted London, 1710.

A Dialogue or New Friendly Debate Between a High and Low Churchman, Concerning Elections: or the Most Certain Rules How to Know and Choose the Fittest Men to Serve in Parliament. London, 1705.

Division Our Destruction: or, a Short History of the French Faction in England. 1st ed. London: John Nutt, 1702.

[Drake, James.] *The History of the Last Parliament ... to Which is Added a Short Defense of the Last Parliament Began at Westminster the tenth ... of February ... 1700.* 1st ed. London: Francis Coggan, Robert Gibson and Thomas Hodgson, 1702.

[———.] *Some Necessary Considerations Relating to All Future Elections of Members To Serve in Parliament, Humbly Offered to All Electors, Whether They Be True Sons of the Church of England ... or Modest Protestant Dissenters....* London, 1702.

England's Corruptions and Mismanagements Discovered in a Dialogue Between Trueman and Legion, Setting Forth the Vitious and Corrupt Practices of Those who Endeavour to Enslave and Resine this Nation and Publicly Exclaim Against Such Worthy Patriots of the House of Commons, and Others who Endeavour to Preserve the Same. N.p., 1702.

Europe a Slave When the Empire Is in Chains: Shewing the Deplorable State of Germany, from the Invasion of the French, and the Fatal Consequence of it to Us and All Europe. 1st ed. London: Ann Baldwin, 1713.

The False Test Set in a True Light: Being a Full Confutation of Two Scandalous Papers, One Entituled, "A Test Offered to the Consideration of the Electors of Great Britain"; the Other Entituled, "A List of the ... Commons That Voted for and Against the Clause of the Hanoverian Succession in the Year 1702," etc. [London]: Jonah Bowyer, 1710.

General Maxims in Trade, Particularly Applied to the Commerce Between Great Britain and France. London: Samuel Buckley, 1713.

[Harley, Robert, and Clement, Simon.] *Faults on Both Sides: or an Essay upon the Original Cause, Progress, and Mischievous Consequences of the Factions in This Nation ... By Way of Answer to the Thoughts of an Honest Tory.* 2nd ed. London: Booksellers of London and Westminster, 1710.

The Hereditary Right of the Crown of England Asserted; the History of the Succession Since the Conquest Clear'd, and the True English Constitution Vindicated from the Misrepresentations of Dr. Higden's "View and Defence," Wherein Some Mistakes Also of our Common Historian are Rectify'd; and Several Particulars Relating to the Succession, and to the Title of the House of Suffolk, are now First Publish'd from Ancient Records and Original MSS. 1st ed. London: George James, 1713.

[Hoadly, Benjamin.] *The Election-Dialogue Between a Gentleman and His Neighbor in the Country, Concerning the Choice of Good Members for the Next Parliament.* 1st ed. London: Ann Baldwin, 1710.

[———.] *The French King's Thanks to the Tories of Great Britain.* [London]: Ann Baldwin, 1710.

[———.] *A Letter of Advice to the Freeholders of England, Concerning the Election of Members To Serve in the Ensuing Parliament.* London: Sarah Popping, 1710.

[———.] *Serious Advice to the Good People of England, Shewing Them Their True Interest and Friends.* London: Ann Baldwin, 1710.

Honest Advice to the Electors of Great Britain in the Present Choice of Their Representatives. London: Benjamin Bragg, [1708].

Honest Clodd's Advice to His Countrymen, How to Chuse Such Members of Parliament at the Next Election as May Preserve Their Liberties and Estates. [London], 1710.

Instructions to the Freeholders Drawn from Her Majesty's ... Speech [July 16, 1713] *to Both Houses of Parliament.* London: Mrs. Smith in Cornhill, 1713.

Jack Presbyter's Downfall: or, the Church in Glory Occasioned by the Dissolution of the Late Parliament; to an Excellent New Tune. London, 1710.

The Judgment of Whole Kingdoms and Nations Concerning the Rights, Powers, and Prerogatives of Kings and the Rights, Privileges and Properties of the People. 10th ed. of *Vox Populi Vox Dei;* London, 1709. London, 1713.

A Letter from a Freeholder of the County of Norfolk, to One of the Knights of the Shire: Occasion'd by Dr. Sacheverell's Tryal. London, 1710.

A Letter from a Gentleman at the Court of St. Germains, to One of His Friends in England. London: John Baker, 1710.

A Letter from a Member of the House of Commons to His Friend in the Country, Relating to the Bill of Commerce. With a True Copy of the Bill and an Exact List of All Those Who Voted for and Against Engrossing the Bill. London: John Baker, 1713.

Letter from Monsieur Pet——m to Monsieur B——ys. Faithfully Translated from the French Original. N.p., 1710.

A Letter to the Freeholders. N.p., [1710].

A Letter to a Friend; Occasion'd by a late Pamphlet; Call'd "Advice to the Electors of Great Britain." London, 1708.

A Letter to a Friend Shewing How Much 'Tis the Interest of Every Elector and Fair Trader To Vote for Such Candidates as Are Against the Eighth and Ninth Articles [of the Treaty of Utrecht] *and Particularly at the Next Ensuing Election of the City of London.* London: John Baker, 1713.

A Letter to a Gentleman Elected a Knight of the Shire to Serve in the Present Parliament. London, 1702.

A Letter to the Gentlemen and Freeholders of the County of Dorset, Concerning the Next Election of Members of Parliament for the Said County. London, 1713.

A Letter to Sir R—— H——, Wherein Is Considered, What Effect the Repeal of Those Laws Which Now Regulate Our Commerce with France Are Likely To Have on the Trade and Manufactures of England. London: Ann Baldwin, 1713.

A Letter to a West Country Clothier and Freeholder Concerning Parliament's Rejecting the French Treaty of Commerce, by

Way of Advice in the Ensuing Elections with a List of Those That Voted for the Bill. [London]: John Baker, 1713.

The Loyal Man's Psalter. N.p., 1713.

[Mackworth, Humphrey.] *Letter from a Member of Parliament to his Friend in the Country Giving a Short Account of the Proceedings of the Tackers.* 5th ed. London, 1705.

[Maynwaring, Arthur.] *Four Letters to a Friend in North Britain, upon the Publishing the Tryall of Dr. Sacheverell.* London, 1710.

[Maynwaring, Arthur, and Churchill, Sarah.] *Advice to the Electors of Great Britain, Occasioned by the Intended Invasion from France.* London: The Heirs of Andrew Anderson, 1708.

The Miseries of England, From the Growing Power of her Domestick Enemies. London, 1702.

The Moderator, or a View of the State of the Controversy Betwixt Whigg and Tory: Short Animadversions on the Picture of a Modern Whigg ... by a True Englishman of No Party. London, 1702.

The Modern Whig Dictator: or, the Exultation. London: Booksellers of London and Westminster, 1702.

A Modest Answer to the Four Immodest Letters to a Friend in North Britain. London, 1710.

A New Test of the Church of England's Loyalty: or Whiggish Loyalty and Church Loyalty Compared. London, 1702.

A New Test of the Church of England's Honesty. London, 1702.

The Observator Observ'd: or; a Scourge for an Ingrateful Rebel to Flaug Him Thru' London Instead of Devonshire.... London: Booksellers of London and Westminster, 1702.

The Oxfordshire Nine: A Poem. London, 1705.

The Perkinite Jacks, or a New Ballad on the Tackers, 11 May, 1705. N.p., [1705].

Plain French: or a Satyr Upon the Tackers. To Which Is Added "The Character of a True Patriot." Written To Caution and Direct English Free-Holders in the Choice of a New Parlia-

ment, and Particularly the Electors in Buckinghamshire. 4th ed. N.p., 1705.

The Politicks of High-Church: or, a System of Their Principles About Government ... Recommended to the Consideration of the Electors Against the Choice of Members for Next Parliament. London, 1705.

Presbyterian Loyalty in two Letters, one Directed to the Moderate Churchman, Mr. Palmer, Author of a "Vindication of the Loyalty," the Other to a Tacking Member of the House of Commons, Giving an Account of the Dissenters' Loyalty.... London: Richard Wilkin, 1705.

The Pretensions of the Church and Its Enemies Stated. London, 1705.

Reasons for a Total Change of a Certain M—— and the Dissolution of P——. London, 1710.

Remarks on a Scandalous Libel Entitl'd: "A Letter from a Member of Parliament" ... Relating to the Bill of Commerce, in Which the Trade with France is Consider'd and the Falsities and Absurdities of the "Mercator" Are Expos'd ... to Which Is Added a Caution to the Freeholders of Great Britain in Their Approaching Elections; and an Exact List of This House of Commons Under Several Distinctions. London: Ann Baldwin, 1713.

The Reviewer Reviewed; or Some Remarks upon the Review. London, 1705.

[Sacheverell, Henry.] *The Political Union, a Discourse Shewing the Dependence of Government on Religion.* 1st ed. Oxford: Leonard Lichfield, 1702.

[———.] *The Rights of the Church of England Asserted and Prov'd.* London: John Knapton, 1705.

[St. John, Henry.] *A Letter to the Examiner.* 1st ed. London, 1710.

A Satyr on the Earl of Oxford, Lord Bolingbroke, Mr. Moor and Mr. Prior. In vol. 11 of the *Harleian Miscellany.* 12 vols. London: R. Dutton, 1808–1811.

Scandal Display'd, or a Word in Season: Being an Answer to ... "Advice to the Electors. ..." [London]: Benjamin Bragg, [1708].

Seasonable Advice to the Electors. London, 1705.

Seasonable Queries Concerning a New Parliament. London, 1710.

A Second Test Offer'd to the Electors of Great Britain. Impartially Collected out of the Addresses of Both Parties. London, 1710.

Seldom Comes a Better: or, a Tale of a Lady and her Servants. 1st ed. London, 1710.

A Serious Address to the Commoners of England Concerning the Approaching Elections of Parliament. London, 1705.

A Short Account of the Expiring Parl[ia]m[e]nt. London: Richard Newcomb, 1713.

"A Short Defence of the Last Parliament" Answer'd Article by Article, to Which Is Added a Paper Called "the Candidates Try'd." London, 1702.

A Short Defence of the Last Parliament with a Word of Advice to All Electors for the Ensuing. London: Elizabeth Mallet, 1701.

Some Cautions Offered to the Consideration of Those Who Chuse Members To Serve in Parliament, to Which Is Added a List of Those Who Voted for and Against the Bill of Commerce. London, 1713.

Some Plain Observations Recommended to the Consideration of Every Honest Englishman; Especially to the Electors of Parliament-Members. [London], 1705.

Les Soupirs de l'Europe, etc., or the Groans of Europe at the Prospect of the Present Posture of Affairs: In a Letter from a Gentleman at the Hague to a Member of Parliament. 1st ed. N.p., 1713.

A Speech Without Doors, Concerning the Most Effectual Way of Providing Forty Thousand Landsmen, as England's Quota in the Present Grand Confederacy. London: Elizabeth Mallet, 1702.

Suffragium: or the Humours of the Electors in Chusing Members for Parliament: a Poem. 1st ed. London: Benjamin Bragg and John Howe, 1702.

A Supplement to the Faults on Both Sides: Containing the Compleat History of the Proceedings of a Party Ever Since the Revolution. 1st ed. London: John Baker, 1710.

The Tackers Toss'd in a Blanket. London, 1705.

The Tackers Vindicated, or an Answer to Whig New Black-List Which Has Been Dispersed Abroad Since the Rising of Both Houses of Parliament. London: Benjamin Bragg, 1705.

The Tacking Club; or a Satyr on Dr. Sacheverell and his Bulleys. N.p., 1710.

A Test Offer'd to the Consideration of the Electors of Great Britain. [London], 1710.

The Testimonies of Several Citizens of Fickleborough in the Kingdom of Fairyland Concerning the Life and Character of Robert Hush, Commonly Called Bob. To Which are prefixed some Memoirs of the Life of Charity Hush, the Grandfather, and of Oliver Hush, the Father of the Said Bob. London: John Morphew, 1713.

This Is the Time: or Serious Advice ... Concerning the Election of Members of Parliament. London, 1710.

Tom Tell-Truths. London, 1705.

True English Advice to the Kentish Freeholders. London, 1710.

The True Picture of a Modern Tory: in a Dialogue Between Jack and Ned, two Agents for the Jacobite Party. London, 1702.

The Trade with France, Italy, Spain, and Portugal Considered: with Some Observations on the Treaty of Commerce Between Great Britain and France. 1st ed. London: John Baker, 1713.

Vox Populi, Vox Dei, Being True Maxims of Government: Proving, I, that all Kings, Governors, and Forms of Government Proceed from the People. 1st ed. London: John Matthews, 1709.

[Walpole, Robert.] *A Short History of the Parliament Which Committed Sir Robert Walpole to the Tower, Expelled him from the*

House of Commons, and Approved of the Infamous Peace of Utrecht. 1st ed. London: T. Warner, 1713.

A Word of Advice to the Citizens of London, Concerning the Choice of Members of Parliament at the Ensuing Election. London, 1705.

B. Periodicals

British Merchant; or Commerce Preserved; in Answer to the Mercator; or Commerce Retrieved. London: Ann Baldwin, 1713–1714.

A Collection from Dyer's Letters Concerning the Elections of the Present Parliament: with an Appendix Relating to Some Other Publick Matters. London: Benjamin Bragg, 1706.

The Englishman, A Political Journal by Richard Steele. Edited by Rae Blanchard. Oxford: Oxford University Press, 1955.

Examiner; or Remarks upon Papers and Occurrences. London: John Barber, 1710–1714.

Flying Post; or the Post Master. London: William Hurt, 1695–1733.

Medley. 1st ser. London: John Baker and Ann Baldwin, 1710–1711.

Mercator; or Commerce Retrieved, Being the Considerations on the State of the British Trade. London: Benjamin Tooke and John Barber, 1713–1714.

Moderator. London: John Morphew, 1710.

Observator. London: Benjamin Bragg and John Howe, 1702–1712.

Post Man and the Historical Account. London: Francis Leach and Dryden Leach, 1695–1730.

Rehearsal of Observator. London: Booksellers of London and Westminster, 1704–1709.

Supplement. London: 1709–1712.

Weekly Review of the Affairs of France. London: John Matthews and John Baker, 1704–1713.

Whig-Examiner. London: Joseph Addison, 1710.

II. Published Documents

Ball, F. Elrington, ed. *The Correspondence of Jonathan Swift*. 6 vols. London: G. Bell and Sons, 1910–1914.

Cartwright, James J., ed. *The Wentworth Papers, 1705–1739: Selected from the Private and Family Correspondence of Thomas Wentworth, Lord Raby*. London: Wyman and Sons, 1883.

Graham, Walter, ed. *Letters of Joseph Addison*. Oxford: Oxford University Press, 1941.

Great Britain. Historical Manuscripts Commission.

Report on the MSS of the Corporation of Chester. Ser. 7, 8th report, pt. 1, sec. ii. London: H. M. Stationery Office, 1881.

Report on the MSS of the Duke of Buccleuch, Montagu House, Whitehall. Ser. 45. London: H. M. Stationery Office, 1903.

Report on the MSS of the Duke of Portland. Ser. 29, 13th and later reports. 7 vols. London: H. M. Stationery Office, 1899–1931.

Report on the MSS of the Earl of Cowper, at Melbourne. Ser. 23, 12th report, Appendixes ii and iii. 2 vols. London: H. M. Stationery Office, 1889.

Report on the MSS of the Earl of Dartmouth. Ser. 20, 12th report, Appendix v. London: H. M. Stationery Office, 1887.

Report on the MSS of the Marquis of Ailesbury. Ser. 43, 15th report, Appendix vii. London: H. M. Stationery Office, 1898.

Report on the MSS of the Marquis of Bath at Longleat, Wiltshire. Ser. 58, 3 vols. London: H. M. Stationery Office, 1904–1909.

Great Britain. Parliament. House of Commons. 1878. Reports and Papers, vol. LXIX, 2 pts. *Members of Parliament: Return to two Orders of the Honourable the House of Commons Dated 4 May 1876 and 9 March 1877.* London: H. Hansard, 1878.

Hill, J. W. F., ed. *The Letters and Papers of the Banks Family of Revesby Abbey, 1704–1760.* Lincoln Record Society Publications, vol. XLV. Hereford: Lincoln Record Society, 1952.

Journals of the House of Commons, 1547–1714. 17 vols. London, 1803.

Journals of the House of Lords, 1578–1714. 18 vols. London, 1846.

Norgate, Fr., ed. "Correspondence between Defoe and John Fransham, of Norwich (1704–1707)." *Notes and Queries,* 5th ser., 3 (April 3, 1875), 260–263.

Parke, Gilbert, ed. *Letters and Correspondence, Public and Private, of Henry St. John, Viscount Bolingbroke.* 2 vols. London: G. G. and J. Robinson, 1798.

Swift, Jonathan. *Journal to Stella.* Edited by Harold Williams. 2 vols. Oxford: Oxford University Press, 1948.

Verney, Margaret Lady, ed. *Verney Letters of the Eighteenth Century from the MSS at Claydon House.* 2 vols. London: Longmans Green, 1930.

III. Secondary Works

Aiken, William A., and Henning, Basil D., eds. *Conflict in Stuart England: Essays in Honour of Wallace Notestein.* New York: New York University Press, 1960.

Allen, Robert J. *The Clubs of Augustan London.* Harvard Studies in English, vol. VII. Cambridge, Mass.: Harvard University Press, 1933.

Bateson, Thomas. "The Relations of Defoe and Harley." *English Historical Review,* 15 (April 1900), 238–250.

Beljame, Alexandre. *Men of Letters and the English Public in the Eighteenth Century, 1660–1744: Dryden, Addison, Pope.* Edited by Bonamy Dobree. London: Routledge and Kegan Paul, 1948.

Bennett, Gareth V. "King William and the Episcopate." In *Essays in Modern English Church History in Memory of Norman Sykes.* Edited by Gareth V. Bennett and J. D. Walsh. Oxford: Oxford University Press, 1966.

Bonner, W. H. "Moll, Knapton, and Defoe: A Note on Early Serial Publication." *Review of English Studies*, 10 (July 1934), 322–323.

Brawner, J. P. "Swift and the Harley–St. John Ministry." *West Virginia University Philological Studies*, 3 (1939), 238–250.

Burnet, Gilbert Bishop. *History of My Own Time.* 6 vols. Oxford: Clarendon Press, 1823.

Burton, I. F., Riley, P. W., and Rowlands, E., "Political Parties in the Reigns of William III and Anne: The Evidence of the Division Lists." *Bulletin of the Institute of Historical Research*, Special Supplement no. 7 (November 1968), 1–72.

Carswell, John. *The Old Cause: Three Biographical Studies in Whiggism.* London: Cresset Press, 1954.

Churchill, Winston S. *Marlborough: His Life and Times.* 4 vols. London: George G. Harrap, 1933–1938.

Cobbett, William. *The Parliamentary History of England from the Norman Conquest in 1066 to 1803.* 36 vols. London: R. Bagshaw, 1806–1820.

Collins, A. S. "Growth of the Reading Public during the Eighteenth Century." *Review of English Studies*, 2 (1926), 284–294, 428–438.

Cook, Richard I. "The Audience of Swift's Tory Tracts, 1710–1714." *Modern Language Quarterly*, 24 (March 1963), 31–41.

———. "'Mr. *Examiner*' and 'Mr. *Review*': The Tory Apologetics of Swift and Defoe." *Huntington Library Quarterly*, 29 (February 1966), 127–146.

———. *Jonathan Swift as a Tory Pamphleteer.* Seattle, Wash.: University of Washington Press, 1967.

Coombs, Douglas. *The Conduct of the Dutch: British Opinion and the Dutch Alliance during the War of the Spanish Succession.* The Hague: M. Nijhoff, 1958.

Cranfield, Geoffrey A. *The Development of the Provincial Newspaper, 1700–1760*. Oxford: Oxford University Press, 1962.

Cunnington, G. Elisabeth, "The General Election of 1705." Master's thesis, University of London, 1938.

Davis, Godfrey. "The Fall of Harley in 1708." *English Historical Review*, 56 (1951), 246–254.

Dickinson, H. T. "The Tory Party's Attitude to Foreigners: A Note on Party Principles in the Age of Anne." *Bulletin of the Institute of Historical Research*, 40 (November 1967), 153–165.

Dictionary of National Biography. Edited by Leslie Stephen and Sidney Lee. 66 vols. 1885–1901. Reprinted (66 vols. in 22). Oxford: Oxford University Press, 1908–1909.

Dottin, Paul. *Daniel Defoe et ses Romans*. 3 vols. Paris: Les Presses Universitaires de France, 1924.

Every, George. *The High Church Party, 1688–1718*. London: Society for Promoting Christian Knowledge, 1956.

Ewald, William B. *Rogues, Royalty and Reporters: The Age of Queen Anne through its Newspapers*. Boston: Houghton Mifflin, 1957.

Feiling, Keith. *A History of the Tory Party, 1640–1714*. Oxford: Clarendon Press, 1924.

Ferguson, Richard S. *Cumberland and Westmorland M.P.'s from the Restoration to the Reform Bill of 1867*. Carlisle: C. Thurman and Sons, 1871.

Fieldhouse, H. N. "Bolingbroke's Share in the Jacobite Intrigue of 1710–1714." *English Historical Review*, 52 (1937), 443–459.

Forrester, Eric G. *Northamptonshire County Elections and Electioneering, 1695–1832*. Oxford: Oxford University Press, 1941.

Furley, O. W. "The Whig Exclusionists: Pamphlet Literature in the Exclusion Campaign, 1679–1681." *Cambridge Historical Journal*, 13 (1957), 19–36.

Geikie, Roderick, and Montgomery, Isabel. *The Dutch Barrier, 1705–1719*. Cambridge: Cambridge University Press, 1930.

Goldgar, Bertrand A. *The Curse of Party: Swift's Relations with*

Addison and Steele. Lincoln, Nebr.: University of Nebraska Press, 1961.

Grego, Joseph. *History of Parliamentary Elections and Electioneering in the Old Days . . . from the Stuarts to Victoria*. London: Chatto and Windus, 1886.

Hanson, Laurence. *Government and the Press, 1695–1763*. Oxford: Oxford University Press, 1936.

Harkness, D. E. A. "The Opposition to the 8th and 9th Articles of the Commercial Treaty of Utrecht." *Scottish Historical Review*, 21 (1923–1924), 219–226.

Hart, A. T. *The Country Priest in English History*. London: Phoenix House, 1959.

———. *The Eighteenth Century Country Parson*. Shrewsbury: Wilding, 1955.

———. *William Lloyd, 1627–1717: Bishop, Politician, Author, and Prophet*. London: Society for Promoting Christian Knowledge, 1952.

Holmes, Geoffry S. *British Politics in the Age of Anne*. New York: St. Martin's, 1967.

Holmes, Geoffry S., and Speck, W. A., eds. *The Divided Society: Parties and Politics in England, 1694–1716*. Documents of Modern History. New York: St. Martin's, 1968.

Horowitz, Henry. *Revolution Politics: The Career of Daniel Finch, Second Earl of Nottingham, 1647–1730*. Cambridge: Cambridge University Press, 1968.

James, Francis G. *North Country Bishop: A Biography of William Nicolson*. New Haven, Conn.: Yale University Press, 1956.

Jones, J. R. *The First Whigs: The Politics of the Exclusion Crisis, 1679–1683*. Oxford: Oxford University Press, 1961.

Latimer, John. *The Annals of Bristol in the Eighteenth Century*. Bristol: privately printed, 1893.

Lecky, William E. *A History of England in the Eighteenth Century*. 7 vols. New York: D. Appleton, 1878–1890.

Macfarlane, John. "Pamphlets and the Pamphlet Duty of 1712." *Library*, n.s., 1 (1900), 298–304.

McInnes, Angus. "The Political Ideas of Robert Harley." *History,* n.s., 50 (October 1965), 309–322.

Morgan, William T. "An Eighteenth Century Election in England." *Political Science Quarterly*, 37 (1922), 585–604.

———. *English Political Parties and Leaders in the Reign of Queen Anne, 1702–1710.* New Haven, Conn.: Yale University Press, 1920.

———. "The Ministerial Revolution of 1710 in England." *Political Science Quarterly*, 36 (1921), 184–210.

Morgan, William T., and Morgan, Chloe S. *Bibliography of British History, 1700–1715.* 5 vols. Bloomington, Ind.: Indiana University Press, 1934–1942.

Nichols, John, ed. *Literary Anecdotes of the Eighteenth Century.* 2nd ed. 9 vols. London: Nichols, Son and Bentley, 1812–1816.

Nulle, Stebelton H. *Thomas Pelham-Holles, Duke of Newcastle: His Early Political Career, 1693–1724.* Philadelphia: University of Pennsylvania Press, 1931.

Ogg, David. *England in the Reigns of James II and William III.* Oxford: Oxford University Press, 1955.

Plumb, John H. "Elections to the House of Commons in the Reign of William III." Dissertation, Cambridge University, 1939.

———. "The Growth of the Electorate in England from 1600 to 1715." *Past and Present,* no. 45 (November 1969), 90–116.

———. *The Growth of Political Stability in England, 1675–1725.* London: Macmillan, 1967.

———. *Sir Robert Walpole: The Making of a Statesman.* Boston: Houghton Mifflin, 1956.

Poston, Lawrence, III. "Defoe and the Peace Campaign, 1710–1713: A Reconsideration." *Huntington Library Quarterly*, 27 (November 1963), 1–20.

Price, J. M. "A Note on the Circulation of the London Press, 1704–1714." *Bulletin of the Institute of Historical Research*, 31 (November 1958), 215–224.

Ransome, Mary. "The General Election of 1710." Master's thesis, University of London, 1938.

———. "The Parliamentary Career of Sir Humphrey Mackworth." *University of Birmingham Historical Journal*, 1 (1948), 232–254.

———. "The Press in the General Election of 1710." *Cambridge Historical Journal*, 6 (1939), 209–221.

———. "Church and Dissent in the Election of 1710." *English Historical Review*, 56 (January 1941), 76–89.

Roscoe, E. S. *Robert Harley, Earl of Oxford, Prime Minister, 1710–1714*. London: Methuen, 1902.

Scudi, Abbie T. *The Sacheverell Affair*. Columbia University Studies in History, Economics, and Public Law, no. 456. New York: Columbia University Press, 1939.

Sharp, Thomas. *The Life of John Sharp, Archbishop of York . . . Collected from his Diary, Letters, etc.* 2 vols. London, 1825.

Snyder, Henry L. "The Circulation of Newspapers in the Reign of Queen Anne." *Library*, 5th ser., 23 (September 1968), 206–235.

———. "Daniel Defoe, Arthur Maynwaring, Robert Walpole, and Abel Boyer: Some Considerations of Authorship." *Huntington Library Quarterly*, 33 (February 1970), 133–153.

———. "Daniel Defoe, the Duchess of Marlborough, and the *Advice to the Electors of Great Britain*." *Huntington Library Quarterly*, 29 (November 1965), 53–62.

———. "The Reports of a Press Spy for Robert Harley: New Bibliographical Data for the Reign of Queen Anne." *Library*, 5th ser., 22 (December 1967), 326–345.

Speck, W. A. "The House of Commons, 1702–1714: A Study in Political Organization." Dissertation, Oxford University, 1965.

———. *Tory and Whig: The Struggle in the Constituencies, 1701–1715*. New York: St. Martin's, 1970.

Stevens, David H. *Party Politics and English Journalism, 1702–1742*. Menasha, Wis.: George Banta, 1916.

Sutherland, James. "The Circulation of Newspapers and Literary Periodicals, 1700–1730." *Library*, 4th ser., 15 (June 1934), 110–124.

———. *Defoe*. 2nd ed. New York: Methuen, 1950.

Sykes, Norman. *Church and State in England in the Eighteenth Century*. Cambridge: Cambridge University Press, 1934.

———. "The General Election of 1705 and the Cathedral Chapter of Exeter." *English Historical Review*, 45 (April 1930), 260–272.

Trevelyan, G. M. *England under Queen Anne*. 3 vols. London: Longmans, Green, 1930–1934.

———. *England under the Stuarts*. 21st ed. London: Methuen, 1949.

———. *The English Revolution, 1688–1689*. London: Thornton Butterworth, 1938.

Troyer, Howard W. *Ned Ward of Grubstreet: A Study of Sub-literary London in the Eighteenth Century*. Cambridge, Mass.: Harvard University Press, 1946.

The Victoria History of the County of Leicester. Edited by W. G. Hoskins. Vol. II. *The Victoria History of the Counties of England*. London: Oxford University Press, 1954.

The Victoria History of the County of Wiltshire. Edited by R. B. Pugh and Elizabeth Crittall. Vol. V. *The Victoria History of the Counties of England*. London: Oxford University Press, 1957.

Walcott, Robert. "English Party Politics (1688–1714)." In *Essays in Modern English History in Honor of Wilbur Cortez Abbott*. Edited by Dorothy K. Clark and others. Cambridge, Mass.: Harvard University Press, 1941.

———. *English Politics in the Early Eighteenth Century*. Harvard Historical Monographs, no. 28. Cambridge, Mass.: Harvard University Press, 1956.

———. "The Idea of Party in the Writing of Later Stuart History." *Journal of British Studies*, I (1962), 54–61.

Wright, Thomas. *Caricature History of the Georges: or Annals of the House of Hanover*. London: John Camden Hotten, 1868.

Index